COOKING
WITH
WHEY

COOKING
WITH
WHEY

**A Cheesemaker's Guide
to Using Whey in**
Probiotic Drinks, Savory Dishes,
Sweet Treats, and More!

CLAUDIA LUCERO

Storey Publishing

The mission of Storey Publishing is to serve our customers by
publishing practical information that encourages
personal independence in harmony with the environment.

Edited by Lisa H. Hiley and Carleen Madigan
Art direction and book design by Erin Dawson
Text production by Jennifer Jepson Smith
Indexed by Andrea Chesman
Illustrations by © Alice Pattullo

Storey books are available at special discounts when purchased in bulk for premi-
ums and sales promotions as well as for fund-raising or educational use. Special
editions or book excerpts can also be created to specification. For details, please
call 800-827-8673, or send an email to sales@storey.com.

STOREY PUBLISHING
210 MASS MoCA Way
North Adams, MA 01247
storey.com

Printed in the United States by Versa Press
10 9 8 7 6 5 4 3 2 1

Library of Congress Cataloging-in-Publication Data on file

Dedicated to Jane

Your stories of Pennsylvania Dutch farm life
and your family's Depression-era recipes made
a big impact on me, as have you and your son.
Thank you for these gifts and so much more.

CONTENTS

How I Made My Way to Whey

I was raised with fresh Mexican cheeses. Nothing made me happier while out grocery shopping with my grandma than visiting the cheese counter for a soft, fresh cheese and then the tortilleria for a steamy corn tortilla. Those simple snacks assembled right there on the street were comfort-food bliss. I was lucky to be allowed/required to cook along with my mom and grandmother from an early age. Working in the kitchen with them, I absorbed the value and reward of cooking traditional foods from scratch.

Several generations of extended family gathered on Sundays to devour the food we made with so much love and care. As I followed this appreciation of good food into adulthood, I came upon cheesemaking and dove in deep. Amazed by my new superpower, I set out to teach others.

In addition to teaching classes, I created a line of three cheese kits for cheeses made in under an hour with one gallon of milk. I started an Etsy shop in 2009 and was soon filling wholesale orders to stores like Whole Foods Market and Williams Sonoma as well as many small businesses. After three years, I left my full-time job at the nonprofit Rock 'n' Roll Camp for Girls and started to write books: first *One-Hour Cheese*, then *One-Hour Dairy-Free Cheese*, and most recently,

Instant Pot Cheese. Being an author allowed me to travel the country on book tours and to teach classes.

More than a decade later, my small business, Urban Cheesecraft, is going strong thanks to loyal customers who want to take some of their food production into their own hands. All along, I have focused publicly on making cheese while privately coming up with a multitude of uses for whey. I am beyond happy to finally tackle the subject so that my customers, students, and hopefully many others can enjoy closing the loop on their homemade dairy production.

About the Recipes

When I set out to take on whey, I wanted to go beyond my own paradigms, skills, and creativity. I am delighted to have included recipes, insights, and uses from a variety of creative people in different fields. I know you will enjoy their recipes and expertise. I certainly have.

Many of the recipes I adapted myself reflect my Mexican roots. There are savory and sweet uses, main dishes, sides, sweets, and beverages. I also enjoy food from all cultures and wanted to include flavors from around the world. When a recipe didn't explicitly use whey but included milk or another liquid that I thought could be replaced with whey, I adapted it. The recipe contributors did the same.

Cuisines travel through history and around the world. In this book you will see influences from Africa, Brazil, France, India, Lebanon, Italy, Japan, Russia, Mongolia, Turkey, Scotland, Iran, Norway, Spain, several regions of the United States, and probably other places I don't even realize. I hope you adapt some of your family's traditional recipes using whey, too.

A Bit of Context

It would feel strange to share this book without mentioning that I wrote it during the initial lockdown phase of the 2020 COVID-19 pandemic. That may explain why I included many sentimental memories— and why no-yeast bread became important! I had to extend my deadlines more than once because it was difficult to develop and test recipes when stores either didn't have enough stock or were setting limits on staples like yeast, milk, eggs, and flour. At the same time, many of my recipe contributors were fighting for their livelihoods and homeschooling their children, not to mention worrying about their own and their family's health, as we all were. I did not want to pepper the book with reminders of the sadness, fear, and upheaval of that time, but the struggles we faced were too important to ignore completely. Suffice to say that it became more critical than ever to avoid waste, to feel self-reliant, and to be creative.

I'm convinced that the challenging circumstances made this book richer in the end. I am nothing if not resourceful, so I managed to create a book despite the obstacles, and one that I am proud of. Testing the recipes comforted me immensely, my household ate well, and we remained healthy. This little time capsule of a book will always be precious to me.

My greatest hope is that this book can influence home cheesemakers, yogurt makers, and the dairy industry to put whey to full use as a resource. I have just scratched at the surface of possibilities. There is so much more that can be done with this useful by-product. My entrepreneurial mind sees many seeds for businesses and innovation. I hope those seeds grow and spread with you. Let's say no to food *wheyst*!

PART 1

THERE'S A LOT TO LEARN ABOUT WHEY

ON AVERAGE, NINE POUNDS OF SWEET WHEY are produced for every pound of cheese, and for every four cups of Greek yogurt, at least one cup of acid whey is created. A single dairy-product plant in Michigan produces 11,000 pounds of whey per hour, every day, all year long. Multiply that by all the cheese found in grocery stores and home refrigerators in the nation, not to mention the entire world! That's a lot of whey, most of which used to be treated as waste and dumped into waterways.

The problem with that is that excessive amounts of whey wreak havoc on life in lakes and ponds. Oxygen levels in the water drop and too much algae grows, blocking sunlight and affecting fish and other wildlife. In 1974 the EPA stepped in to prevent the large-scale disposal of commercial whey. As an alternative to sending excess whey to wastewater treatment plants, companies have had to look for more creative methods to dispose of it, which include agricultural uses as animal feed and fertilizer and developing nutritional supplements, such as whey protein powder, for both human and animal consumption.

At least 3,400 patents for whey-based innovations have been filed, but for the most part, the patents are not meant for small operations. So, if whey is so dense in nutrients that its disposal causes problems and so nutrient rich that it makes money for big businesses with value-added products, there are plenty of reasons for us to use it at home.

Whey Use through the Ages

If you think about it, whey is recycled water, in that milk-producing animals need water to create milk for their young, adding many nutrients in the process. For nomadic tribes and other people living in arid environments, whey can be an important source of liquid, especially where clean water is hard to come by. The health benefits of probiotic-rich, fermented whey from cultured raw milks have been recognized for many centuries by people all over the world.

Hippocrates prescribed whey for several ailments, and it was recommended by doctors in the Middle Ages. By the mid-nineteenth century there were more than 400 "whey houses" in Western Europe serving up whey cures. There were even spas throughout Europe in the 1940s that used daily doses of whey as health tonics. While I don't claim that the whey recipes in this book will cure diseases, I hope you find them useful, fun, and above all delicious.

PLASTIC? NO, WHEY!

I find it fascinating and hopeful that the WHEYPACK project, a collaboration between groups in Spain and Portugal, has figured out how to make biodegradable plastic from whey by using yeast to break down the lactose in whey. The whey is sourced from a cheesemaker based in Spain, Central Quesera Montesinos, and the bioplastics are used to package their products. This sustainable production loop has a far lower carbon footprint than petroleum-based packaging material, and it appears to have application potential beyond the dairy industry.

Types of Whey

Whey comes in three basic types, depending on the cheesemaking process: acid, sweet, and cooked. The appearance and viscosity vary, from clear and watery cooked whey to cloudy and milky sweet whey to the almost syruplike quality of acid whey. In addition, each type of whey has its own degree of sweetness and tang, not to mention the nuance of the flavor of the milk that was used. Whether you use milk from cows, goats, or sheep (or even horses or camels!) is generally a matter of preference and availability, not a key factor in any given recipe. (To learn about the nutrient profiles of the different types of whey, see the Appendix, page 116.)

Whey is used strategically in place of vinegar, milk, juice, water, broth, and cheese in the recipes in this book. It feels more familiar when thought of in this way, not to mention quite fun if you like to play mad scientist. Whey can even be used in your garden (see page 24) and incorporated into your skincare routine (see page 26).

I grappled a bit with these definitions because, while I did not want to get needlessly technical, it's important to be clear. Talking about the different types of whey can be confusing, but some recipes require a certain type of whey to work. For example, although whole-milk ricotta is made with the addition of an acid such as lemon juice or vinegar to create curds and whey, the resulting whey is not called "acid whey." It is "cooked whey" (also called deproteinized whey) because the milk has been cooked to a high heat. Acid whey earns

TYPES OF WHEY AND KEY PROPERTIES

Type of Whey	How It's Produced	Properties and Flavor	Notes
ACID WHEY	Acid whey comes primarily from straining yogurt and homemade kefir (not store-bought); also from making some cultured cheeses (quark, cream cheese, some cottage cheeses).	This cultured, fermented whey is full of probiotics. Its tangy flavor comes from the lactic acid excreted by the bacteria that convert the lactose in the milk. The acid isn't added; it develops during the fermentation process. Acid whey is thicker than other types, with an almost syrupy quality.	You can cook with it, but it is best used for cold and frozen applications, which leave the live probiotics intact for a nice gut boost. When it is used in recipes that call for heating the whey, it may need to be clarified (see page 22).
SWEET WHEY	Sweet whey is created when making most cheeses with rennet and cultures or rennet and citric acid (like quick mozzarella).	It tastes milky and mild when fresh but will develop a more acidic flavor after a few days. This cloudy liquid adds a nice richness to recipes.	Sweet whey may need to be clarified (see page 22) for use in beverages or to prevent curds or grit from forming when heated.
COOKED WHEY	Cooked whey results from processes where milk is heated close to or at the boiling point and then an acid such as lemon juice, vinegar, or citric acid is added to separate the curds. Ricotta and paneer are examples of this process.	The taste of the particular acid used might be detectable with a strong flavor like distilled white vinegar, but the tang is usually mild compared to acid whey and the flavor easy to disguise. Because the high heat extracts more protein, cooked whey is the least nutritious; it is also called deproteinized whey.	This is a nice, clear whey that works well for cocktails or making broth. Just be sure to strain it thoroughly through a couple of layers of fine-mesh cheesecloth before using it.
Whey Wannabe: **BUTTERMILK**	Real buttermilk comes from making butter, unlike the thick, white store-bought variety. It can be used in place of whey in some recipes.	It is clear like whey and has some of the taste and texture of low-fat milk. It tastes tangy if cultured, sweet if not.	You can use cultured buttermilk in place of acid whey and fresh buttermilk in place of sweet whey.
Whey Wannabe: **MOZZARELLA LIQUID**	The water (or whey) that is used while stretching mozzarella winds up containing a certain amount of cream.	Like real buttermilk, it somewhat resembles low-fat milk.	If you have a lot of liquid, you can cool it and skim the cream to make butter! Or use it in place of sweet whey in recipes.

its name from the lactic acid that produces it; no cultures or bacteria are added.

It's true that acid is added or created in every type of cheese, so it might seem logical that all whey would be acidic, but that isn't the determining factor. Technically speaking, sweet whey has a pH greater than or equal to 5.6, whereas acid whey has a pH as low as 3.6. To understand that in some context, whole cow's milk has a pH of about 6.7 and distilled white vinegar has a pH of about 2.5.

A word of warning: Whey contains lactose. Acid whey has less lactose than sweet whey does, but if you are lactose intolerant or have difficulty digesting dairy products, the world of whey for culinary uses may not be for you.

Which Whey to Use?

As I tested different whey types in different uses, I noted the ones that worked best in each recipe. My goal was to find the whey type whose qualities enhanced the outcome. Not all whey types worked for all applications. That was sometimes due to a technical reason like bacterial activity and residual solid content, and sometimes it was simply because of a strong flavor that I did not think complemented the finished product.

For example, I don't love using goat's milk whey to make pudding or ice pops because I find the slight barnyard taste overpowers other flavors. You may love that flavor or not even detect it! I do like goat's milk whey for risotto, soups, and potato salad, and I think it would be fun to experiment with, say, a watermelon-mint granita using whey from a goat's milk feta.

You can assume that the default whey for these recipes came from cow's milk, unless otherwise noted. I did test sheep's milk whey and goat's milk whey, but I did not have access to other types.

As you use whey more often, you will begin to think of it as an ingredient like a seasoned stock or nuanced cheese with unique flavors. When you find yourself with a specific whey on your hands, you'll know which recipe to turn to. Just like goat cheese is classically great with beets, and orange juice magically combines with ice cream to make homemade Creamsicles, a world of whey flavor pairings will start to open up for you.

Just be aware that no recipe will completely disguise a strongly flavored whey. It's the same as knowing that fish stock isn't a great base for making smoothies! In that case, think about using the whey to make treats for your dog (see Going to the Dogs, page 16) or experiment with it as a skincare treatment (Ashley's Rosewater Bath, page 26). You can also use excess whey to treat fungus on plants or just add it to the compost pile (see Garden Uses for Whey, page 24).

An At-a-Glance Guide

You will find the guide at the right with every recipe for quick reference so that you can easily see which types of whey work in a given recipe. If you don't have the "best" whey, I encourage you to taste the one you do have. In most cases, if the flavor is rated "good" or neutral, you can go ahead and use it. In some cases, it will be okay, if diluted, for example. In rare cases, a particular whey just won't work for that recipe.

When acid whey is listed as the only choice, it's because the live cultures in it are necessary for the recipe to work. For example, the lactic acid in a fermented whey creates carbonation in beverages and reacts with baking soda to leaven bread. If there is another option or work-around, I will tell you.

BEST. The ideal whey type for that recipe. In the recipes provided by other makers, it is the one they used to develop the recipe.

GOOD. Will work fine in that recipe but may break with cultural traditions or expectations for flavor and texture.

OKAY. Can be used in a particular recipe if it is all you have, but expect stronger flavors and possible cloudiness. You can always dilute the whey with water to your taste.

NO WAY. Something about this type of whey, perhaps excess salt, acidity, or bacterial activity, is likely to ruin the recipe. (This is rarely the case.)

WHICH WHEY?
BEST Acid
GOOD Sweet
OKAY Cooked

Look for this guide by the ingredients list to learn which type of whey works best for each recipe.

Going to the Dogs

Farmers have fed whey to pigs and chickens throughout history. It's a perfect system in which a by-product from one animal nourishes other animals that will eventually become food for the family. In fact, in Parma, Italy, whey from Parmigiano-Reggiano is fed to pigs that will become Parma ham.

We can do this on a small scale in our own homes, even if we don't have farm animals to share our whey with. I share my home with just one animal: Tutti, a 10-pound Chihuahua/Jack Russell type of mutt. She didn't come to me very food motivated, but in this house that seems to be how we all end up! I had to include a couple of whey uses for her and other canine companions.

Note: Cats are often lactose intolerant, and it's possible that some dogs are as well. If you have never tested dairy with your dog(s), offer them a little whey before making these treats. (And you didn't hear this from me, but you can use bone broth instead if in doubt.)

CONFETTI PUPSICLES

The colorful veggie confetti makes these icy snacks a festive treat for a special occasion, a reward after a visit to the vet, or just because you love your dog! The fishy smell and flavor are sure to be a hit, but these treats are messy as they melt, so only feed them to your dog outdoors. And don't overdo the servings—one or two at a time is enough.

1 cup whey (any, unsalted)

2 canned sardines (packed in water)

¼ cup diced carrot, raw or steamed

½ cup peas, fresh or frozen

1 Pulse the whey and sardines in a blender to the consistency of a chunky smoothie.

2 Distribute the carrots and peas evenly in an ice cube tray. Pour the sardine-whey mixture over them, leaving a little space at the top.

3 Freeze for 3 hours or until solid. Remove from the ice cube tray and store in a covered container. Use within 4 months.

PUPPY PANCAKES

Yes, these tiny pancakes are ridiculously cute, but this recipe made the cut because it doesn't contain wheat or other grains that some dogs are sensitive to, meaning I don't have to buy fancy (expensive) grain-free dog biscuits. Plus they cook in a flash, and most importantly, Tutti loves them. I keep a container of them in the freezer—they break easily for smaller treats. Feel free to change up the banana for mashed sweet potato or pumpkin purée, or use a quarter cup mashed blueberries or shredded apple.

1 **cup chickpea flour**

2 **tablespoons peanut butter**

½ **cup mashed banana**

1 **cup whey (any, unsalted)**

Coconut oil or ghee for frying

1 Combine the flour with the peanut butter and banana in a medium bowl.

2 Add ½ cup of the whey and mix thoroughly. Chickpea flour can vary in absorbency, so you may not need all of the whey or you may need more (you can use milk or broth if you don't have enough whey). Add more of the whey a little at a time until the consistency is like pancake batter.

3 Let the mixture stand for 2 to 3 minutes to allow it to thicken. Heat a skillet or griddle over medium heat.

4 Coat the skillet lightly with oil and drop a heaping tablespoon of batter to test the pancake size. Drop in more batter to make more pancakes in whatever size you like.

5 Cook the pancakes until the tops look slightly opaque and lightly cooked, about 3 minutes. They will not show little bubbles like typical pancakes. Flip and cook for another 2 minutes.

Let the pancakes cool completely before you share a couple with your furry buddy. Freeze the rest in a sealed container. Use within 4 months.

Making Whey

You may already have your own steady source of whey, which means you are probably ready to jump right into the recipes. If that is not the case, or if you want to try something new, here are some basic methods for creating every type of whey used in this book. Do not be intimidated—even if you only learn to make acid whey by draining store-bought yogurt and cooked whey from making whole-milk ricotta, you will be able to make all the recipes in this book.

And don't worry, if you have produced a lot of whey but don't have time to make anything with it right away, you can freeze it!

FREEZING

I often freeze whey right in the container the milk or yogurt originally came in. This is perfect because with the solids removed, there is space in the container to allow for the expansion that will happen in the freezer. If you use a different container, make sure you leave at least 10 percent space at the top (20 percent is even safer). This is especially important with glass, which can crack when the whey freezes and expands.

Use frozen whey within 6 months. If it smells off, like rancid fat, when you thaw it, add it to the compost pile (see page 24).

EQUIPMENT YOU NEED

If you already make cheese, yogurt, and kefir, your kitchen is likely well stocked with the basics. Here are a few items you'll need.

- Heavy-bottomed pots, ranging in capacity from 1 quart to 1 gallon

- Strainer and/or colander for straining whey to remove curd

- Widemouthed funnel

- Heat-resistant storage containers, such as half-gallon and 1-quart canning jars, with lids

- Blender or food processor

- Fine-mesh cheesecloth (90# or 120# thread count) or nut-milk bags for extra-fine straining (Do not use the disposable grocery store variety of cheesecloth with large holes. In a pinch, you can use a lint-free cotton tea towel.)

- Silicone (or other heat-resistant material) scraper or spatula

Acid Whey
from Yogurt or Kefir

Draining yogurt is one of the easiest methods of extracting whey, and the resulting whey is filled with the same beneficial bacteria and tang as the yogurt itself. The yield is low compared to the amount gathered from making cheese, however—about a cup of whey per quart of yogurt.

Acid whey is tangy and flavorful, with a syrupy consistency. This whey is alive with beneficial bacteria as long as it is not heated. If it is heated, it still contains lactic acid and its lactose has been broken down considerably, but it will not ferment other foods. Kefir whey also contains yeasts from the grains used to culture the milk.

ACID WHEY FROM YOGURT

YIELD **About 1 cup whey and 2–3 cups yogurt cheese**

TIME **8–24 hours**

INGREDIENTS
   1 quart yogurt

1   Line a colander with a double layer of fine-mesh cheesecloth and set it over a bowl to catch the whey. Place the yogurt in the colander. You can twist the cheesecloth into a bag and hang the yogurt over a bowl for more rapid draining.

2   Drain overnight or longer. You can strain the yogurt to the thickness of Greek yogurt in 8 hours or yogurt cream cheese in 24 hours.

Store the whey and yogurt in the refrigerator until you are ready to use them. The yogurt and whey will keep for at least 2 weeks or you can freeze whey for up to 6 months.

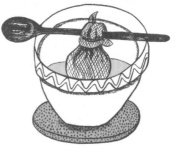

ACID WHEY FROM KEFIR

Kefir whey generally appears as a surprise for most people. They accidentally leave the milk to ferment with kefir grains for a little longer than intended, or the weather is a little warmer than usual and the curd separates from the whey on its own, right in the jar. When you do this intentionally, you end up with kefir curds and whey instead of a milky beverage. You can also use cooked whey instead of milk in this recipe to make a probiotic-rich kefir-style acid whey.

YIELD About 1 cup whey and 3 cups kefir cheese
TIME 24–48 hours
INGREDIENTS

> **1 quart milk**

3–4 tablespoons kefir grains

1 Place the milk in a jar with the kefir grains. Cover and allow to ferment at room temperature for 12 to 24 hours, or until you see a separation between the chunky white solids and the yellow whey. It may be necessary to "burp" the jar by opening and resealing the lid every 8 hours or so because carbon dioxide (fizz!) will accumulate.

2 Line a colander with a double layer of fine-mesh cheesecloth and set it over a bowl. If the kefir grains have floated to the top of the jar, scoop them out. Gently pour the kefir curds and whey into the colander. Remove any remaining grains.

3 Drain the whey for 1 hour, or until it stops actively dripping. The liquid and cheese will both contain probiotic bacteria and that same kefir flavor. They may feel fizzy on your tongue. You can salt the cheese, and add spices or herbs for a tasty dip or, if it is on the thinner side, salad dressing.

The whey and kefir cheese will keep in the refrigerator for at least 2 weeks. You can freeze the whey for up to 6 months.

Cooked Whey
from Ricotta

The two methods for making cooked whey are based on the process of making ricotta.

COOKED WHEY FROM WHOLE-MILK RICOTTA

This whole-milk ricotta recipe yields much more ricotta than the whey-based recipe that follows and gives about the same amount of whey. The ricotta will be slightly crumbly. Avoid using ultra-pasteurized milk when making cheese. Raw milk or common pasteurized milk will give you sure success.

YIELD **About 3 quarts whey and 2 cups ricotta**

TIME **1 hour**

INGREDIENTS

- **1 gallon whole milk**
- **½ cup lemon juice, apple cider vinegar, or citric acid solution (1 teaspoon citric acid dissolved in ½ cup water)**
- **½ teaspoon sea salt**

1 Cook the whey in a pot over medium-high heat until it is frothy and steamy and reaches 185°F (85°C). Stir often to prevent scorching. For the highest yield of cheese and the clearest whey, bring the milk to a boil. Remove from the heat.

2 Stir in the acid. Allow the curds to form in the hot whey for 10 minutes. Do not stir.

3 Line a colander with a double layer of fine-mesh cheesecloth and set it over a bowl. Pour the curds and whey into the colander. Drain until the whey stops actively dripping, 10 to 15 minutes.

4 Transfer the drained ricotta to a bowl and stir in the salt, adding more to taste. Allow the whey to cool before pouring it into a storage container.

TIP: Leaving the milk out at room temperature for an hour will save heating time in step 1.

The whey and ricotta will keep for 1 week in the refrigerator. You can freeze the whey for up to 6 months.

COOKED WHEY FROM WHEY-BASED RICOTTA

In Italy it is common for mozzarella vendors to also sell ricotta because the two products go hand in hand. The word *ricotta* means "re-cooked," and traditional ricotta is made by further cooking the sweet whey from rennet-based cheeses like mozzarella that are heated at low temperatures, such as 105°F (40°C).

This process produces about three tablespoons of ricotta per half gallon of whey. I realize that isn't much enticement as far as cheese goes, but you will also wind up with a good amount of clear, cooked whey, which is useful for recipes where any solids are undesirable, such as sodas, caramel, or puddings. You can also use this technique to clarify any type of whey, though the resulting solids might not be quite as tasty as ricotta.

YIELD **About 3 quarts whey and 3 tablespoons ricotta**

TIME **1 hour**

INGREDIENTS

> **3 quarts sweet whey from a rennet-based cheese such as Fromage Blanc (page 23)**
>
> **2 tablespoons lemon juice, apple cider vinegar, or citric acid solution (½ teaspoon citric acid dissolved in ¼ cup water)**

1 Cook the whey in a pot over medium-high heat until it is frothy and steamy and reaches 195°F (90°C). You may see curds form at the top before adding the acid because the whey contains acid from the previous cheesemaking process. Remove from the heat.

2 Stir in the acid to extract as much curd as possible and ensure that your whey is deproteinized. Skim off the tender curd with a fine-mesh sieve as it forms and transfer it into a colander lined with a double layer of fine-mesh cheesecloth set over a large bowl.

3 Drain until the whey stops actively dripping. This can take a while because this is a small and delicate curd that may clog the cheesecloth. You can rock the colander back and forth or gently scrape the inside of the cheesecloth if you want to hurry it along.

The whey and ricotta will keep in the refrigerator for 1 week, and you can freeze the whey for up to 6 months.

Sweet Whey
from Fromage Blanc

Fromage blanc, made with cow's milk, is the most basic rennet-based cheese one can make, and it is also delicious and versatile. Making it with goat's milk instead results in chèvre, which is equally delicious and versatile. This recipe yields a good three quarts of rich, sweet whey that is mild in flavor and very useful for many of the whey-based creations in this book.

Use common pasteurized milk or raw milk instead of ultra-pasteurized milk when making cheese.

FROMAGE BLANC/CHÈVRE

YIELD About 3 quarts whey

TIME 1 hour

INGREDIENTS

- 1 gallon whole cow's milk or goat's milk (not ultra-pasteurized)
- ¼ cup live starter: cultured buttermilk or unsweetened yogurt or kefir
- ¼ tablet vegetarian rennet dissolved in ¼ cup cool unchlorinated water or ¼ teaspoon liquid rennet (not double strength)
- 1 teaspoon sea salt

1 Warm the milk in a pot over medium heat until it reaches 90°F (32°C). Remove from the heat. Add the starter and stir thoroughly. Add the rennet and stir with a large spoon up, down, and all around about 10 times. Cover the pot and let sit for 12 hours.

2 After 12 hours, the milk should look like thick yogurt or a solid custard. You may see cracks with yellow whey peeking through. Cut the curd across the pot into slices ½ inch thick, then cut in the other direction to create a grid.

continued on next page

3 Line a colander with a double layer of fine-mesh cheesecloth and place it over a bowl large enough to catch the whey. Ladle shallow scoops of curd into the colander until most of it is out of the pot. Gently pour the whey and any remaining bits of curd into the colander.

4 Cover the colander with the pot lid or a plate and let sit at room temperature (72–78°F/22–25°C) for 8 hours, or until the cheese reaches your desired texture. It will thicken more when refrigerated.

5 Transfer the cheese to a storage container and stir in the salt. You can form the cheese into rounds, logs, or wheels and roll them in herbs, spices, or edible flowers. Allow the whey to cool before transferring to a storage container.

The whey and fromage blanc will keep in the refrigerator for 1 week, and you can freeze the whey for up to 6 months.

GARDEN USES FOR WHEY

If you search "whey and agriculture" online, you will enter a rabbit hole of studies conducted by dairy councils, universities, environmental organizations, and government agencies throughout the world on using whey as a soil amendment, fertilizer, fungicide, and more, dating back to the 1960s.

One promising line of research focuses on whey's usefulness against certain root-knot nematodes. These microscopic roundworms lay their eggs in the roots of vegetable plants, decimating crops. In one study, whey was applied via drip irrigation to tomato plants, resulting in 70 percent less root damage compared to untreated plants. That's practically a superpower!

Here are some simple methods for using excess whey in your garden.

COMPOST IT

The same components that make whey work as a fertilizer enable it to help kickstart activity in your compost. Just follow a few rules of thumb to keep your pile balanced. Add enough whey for moisture but not so much that there is seepage. You don't want a pool of whey to collect. Turn the pile when you add the whey and add leaves and other brown matter to balance it.

THERE'S A LOT TO LEARN ABOUT WHEY

FIGHT POWDERY MILDEW

As a novice gardener in a wet growing environment, I made the mistake of planting three grapevines in partial shade on the north side of the house where they don't get enough sun and are susceptible to mildew. I had heard of spraying milk on zucchini plants with powdery mildew, so I thought trying whey as a foliar fungicide was worth a shot.

It didn't take care of all the mildew, but the first year I tried it I picked my largest grape harvest in seven years. I get better results when I start spraying preventively well before mildew settles in. Sweet and acid whey work the best; cooked whey is just okay. You can use frozen and thawed whey, but don't use salted whey—your plants won't like it!

I started with a 50/50 whey/water solution, but it smelled a little too cheesy and attracted flies on hot days. I found that a 20 percent whey solution works nicely. For my three grapevines, 2 cups of whey mixed with 8 cups of water is enough; adjust the amount to suit your needs. Strain the whey before mixing it with the water. (The solids don't hurt the plants or soil but might attract rodents and clog the sprayer.)

Fill a spray bottle with the mixture and apply it liberally anywhere you see mildew or have seen it in the past. You may want to start by spraying just one plant or a small area as a test. I spray weekly during dry spells and reapply after it rains. Mix up a fresh batch each time.

USE IT AS FERTILIZER

I began to use whey as a fertilizer when my homegrown tomatoes and zucchini in my garden developed blossom-end rot. I did some research and found that a lack of calcium in the soil could be to blame. It made sense; we get so much rain here in the Pacific Northwest that it's difficult to keep minerals in the soil. Well, I thought, I know what has calcium: whey!

It worked; I haven't seen blossom-end rot on my veggies since. A wonderful side effect of using whey as fertilizer is that by building up your soil, you protect against fungal overgrowth, too.

Notes: The sodium in salted whey can disrupt your soil's nutrient balance. If the whey you are using is very sour or not fresh, use the proportions given below for acid whey. Too much acidity in your soil can damage your plants rather than help them.

Proportions

- **2 parts sweet or cooked whey to 2 parts water**

- **1 part acid whey to 3 parts water**

Mix the whey with the water and use immediately. To create a low-tech slow-drip system, drill a small hole in the bottom of a bucket or poke a hole in a plastic milk jug, then set the container near the base of the plant. I typically split 1 gallon of mixture between two tomato or zucchini plants, using one milk jug per plant. Water your plants this way every two weeks.

ASHLEY'S ROSEWATER BATH

Once you start to dig into the past and present uses of milk and milk derivatives for skincare, a whole new world opens up, especially when it comes to lactic acid as a natural moisturizer and exfoliant. This is another subject that I could spend a lot more time on, but I only have so many pages in this book, so here is one recipe for a surprising use for excess whey.

Ashley English and I met when she highlighted my business in her book *Home Dairy*. It is part of her Homemade Living series that also includes *Home Apothecary*, from which this recipe was adapted. Ashley works hard on her homestead, so it makes me happy to know that this self-care bath is part of her repertoire.

The whey in this bath is moisturizing and the lactic acid is a mild natural exfoliant. The rose water and honey add soothing qualities and a lovely scent. After a luxurious and therapeutic soak, you will feel like ancient royalty, even if you spent the afternoon cleaning out the chicken coop.

Use as needed, whenever your skin feels dry and parched. Make the mixture just before your bath.

Ingredients

- 3 cups sweet or acid whey (cooked whey is okay)
- 2 tablespoons raw honey
- 2 tablespoons rose water

Warm the whey in a small pan over low heat until just warm to the touch. Remove from the heat. Add the honey and rose water and whisk until fully incorporated.

Fill a bath with warm water. Add the whey mixture to the bath and stir the water with your hand to disperse it. To get the most benefit, soak for at least 10 to 15 minutes.

Gently pat your skin dry with a towel. It's best not to rinse off after coming out of the bath so that the whey continues absorbing into the skin.

SHOWER VERSION: I tried Ashley's bath mixture in a warm shower. I cut the recipe in half and poured the warm whey mixture into a widemouthed jar. I then used a washcloth to apply the mixture as an exfoliating body wash. My skin felt noticeably softer.

If you have sensitive skin, try a patch test on your inner wrist overnight first, or stick to the bath, where the mixture is more diluted.

PART 2

RECIPES

Beverages

You can use whey in place of water, milk, or even yogurt for any beverage that might benefit from a creamy or tangy flavor and a luscious texture. As a substitute for water, whey will improve the character and nutrition of the beverage. Used in place of milk or yogurt, whey lightens the fat content and calorie count. Fermented acid whey from yogurt or kefir enriches an enjoyable drink with probiotics and lactic acid tang.

Orange Wheylius

This drink is inspired by the orange-flavored shopping mall beverage that's not quite a milkshake and not quite a smoothie. I was interested to learn that it was invented in 1929 with the goal of creating an orange juice that was gentler on the stomach. For those of us who are feeling nostalgic, I've re-created a lower-sugar version of that citrus dream using frozen oranges and whey. The whey adds creaminess as well as froth. If you find orange juice too acidic, this might just work for you as was originally intended. I like to include a small piece of orange peel for extra-zesty flavor.

YIELD 1 serving ••• **TIME** 5 hours, 5 minutes active

INGREDIENTS

2–3   navel oranges

      2-inch piece orange zest

1   cup whey

1   teaspoon vanilla extract

1   tablespoon sugar or sugar substitute, optional

2–3   ice cubes, optional

WHICH WHEY?
BEST Sweet, acid
OKAY Cooked

1 Use a vegetable peeler to remove a 2-inch strip of zest from one of the oranges and set it aside. Then peel the oranges and cut them into quarters, removing any seeds. Freeze the pieces in a covered container for at least 5 hours.

2 Blend the frozen orange pieces and zest, whey, vanilla, and sugar, if desired, until creamy and frothy. Taste and add more sweetener, if you want it sweeter. For an even icier drink, add a couple of ice cubes to the blender.

This recipe is easily scaled up to make a whole pitcher to share. It's best enjoyed immediately.

Brazilian Limeade

While this traditional limeade often contains sugar *and* sweetened condensed milk, here we make a lighter version that is no less delicious and rich tasting. The whey will add body and froth up nicely in the blender, making this limeade silky and foamy just like the original. Blending the lime with the peel results in the limiest limeade you've ever had. I like to whip this up as a midday treat when working from home, but it's easily scaled up to make a whole pitcher to share.

YIELD 2 servings

INGREDIENTS

- 1 juicy lime
- 2 cups water
- ½ cup whey
- 2 tablespoons sugar
- Ice for serving

WHICH WHEY?
BEST Sweet, acid
OKAY Cooked

1 Wash the lime, cut off the ends, and cut into quarters (remember we are leaving the peel on!). Remove the seeds.

2 Blend the lime pieces with the water, whey, and sugar until frothy. Taste, and blend in a little more sugar if you want it sweeter. Strain through a fine-mesh sieve. Serve over lots of ice.

Store in the refrigerator and drink within 5 days.

Whey-Torade Recovery Drink

The color of whey always makes me think of yellow sports drinks, so it's fitting that whey has been used as a recovery drink in traditional medicine for as long as dairy products have been part of our diet. With this version, there's no need for artificial colors, synthetic vitamins, high-fructose corn syrup, or other processed ingredients.

A good recovery drink replaces electrolytes lost by prolonged exertion, excessive sweating, or sometimes a stomach bug. Whey contains sodium, various vitamins, and electrolytes including potassium, calcium, and magnesium, making it a perfect way to refuel and rehydrate. The lactose in whey is a natural sugar, supplemented here with honey or maple syrup. Though we often vilify sugars, after a workout they are quickly converted to glucose, which helps muscles recover.

Levels of nutrients vary with each type of whey (see page 116); this base recipe has been formulated to help with recovery no matter which whey you choose.

YIELD 1 quart

INGREDIENTS

- 4 cups whey, chilled
- 3 tablespoons honey or maple syrup
- 2 tablespoons apple cider vinegar or lemon juice
- 1 teaspoon mineral-rich sea salt
- 1 cup cherry juice, orange juice, or another nutritious juice for extra flavor, optional

WHICH WHEY?
BEST Acid, sweet
GOOD Cooked

1 If you are using a rich sweet whey, strain it through a double layer of fine-mesh cheesecloth to remove all the solids.

2 Mix all the ingredients in a pitcher and serve cold. For sports recovery, drink a cup within an hour after your workout.

Store in the refrigerator and drink within 4 days.

Ginger Barley Water

You may have come across a reference to barley water in an old British movie or novel. This historic elixir was used in ancient Greece and is still a favorite health remedy in India. Barley contains soluble fiber, antioxidants, folate, iron, copper, and manganese and is used to boost energy and help with rehydration. Some people claim that it helps with cholesterol and blood sugar imbalances, urinary tract infections, catarrh, and many other ailments.

The barley provides a texture much like that of oat milk, which, along with the velvety mouthfeel of whey, makes this a drink with some substance. I put my spin on it with ginger and lemon, and it quickly became a favorite pick-me-up. You can enjoy this hot or cold. I like having a small cup between lunch and dinner. You can switch up the flavors—try orange peel and a cinnamon stick, for instance.

YIELD 4 servings ••• **TIME** 30 minutes

INGREDIENTS

- 4   cups whey
- ½   cup pearl barley
-     Thumb-size piece fresh ginger, diced
- 2   tablespoons lemon juice
-     2-inch piece lemon zest, no pith
- ¼   cup honey
-     Pinch sea salt

WHICH WHEY?
BEST Sweet
GOOD Cooked
OKAY Acid

1 Combine the whey, barley, ginger, lemon juice, and lemon zest in a 2-quart saucepan and bring to a boil. Lower the heat and simmer for 20 minutes, stirring occasionally, until the barley grains are soft but not mushy.

2 Strain through a fine-mesh sieve. (Or don't— some people leave the grains in. Think of them as boba pearls!)

3 Add the honey and salt and stir thoroughly.

Taste and add more honey if you want it sweeter. Store in the refrigerator and drink within 5 days.

Don't waste that cooked barley. You can add it to soups or top it with veggies and an egg for a savory breakfast.

Golden Whey

This soothing drink—along with its inspiration, golden milk—gets its name from the turmeric that is a key ingredient in the original anti-inflammatory beverage from India. Sometimes golden milk goes by the name turmeric latte in the US. In this version, I use whey instead of milk, of course, and add extra spices to make it a masala chai–inspired hybrid.

The golden hues of the spices, the honey, and the whey are a perfect match. I recommend using whole spices for best flavor, especially the ginger, cinnamon, and cardamom. It's nice to make a double batch so you can warm some up whenever you crave a comforting cup.

YIELD 4 servings ••• **TIME** 20 minutes

INGREDIENTS

- 4 cups whey
- 1 tablespoon freshly grated turmeric root or ground turmeric
- 1 tablespoon chopped fresh ginger or ½ teaspoon ground ginger
- 1 large cinnamon stick or ½ teaspoon ground cinnamon
- 5 cracked cardamom pods or ½ teaspoon ground cardamom
- 2 whole cloves
- 4 teaspoons honey

WHICH WHEY?
BEST Sweet, cooked
OKAY Acid

1 Simmer the whey with the spices in a small pot over low heat for 15 minutes.

2 Remove from the heat and stir in the honey until dissolved, adding more if desired.

3 Strain into mugs and serve warm.

Store in the refrigerator and drink within 5 days.

~~~~~~~~~~~~~~~~~~~~~~~~~~~~~~~~~~~

For a quick, super-simple version, vigorously stir ½ teaspoon ground turmeric and ¼ teaspoon ground ginger into 1 cup hot whey. Sweeten with honey to taste.

Agua Fresca de Melón
(Mexican Cantaloupe Drink)

Street-side taco stands in Mexico greet you with a colorful variety of giant glass jugs, each holding a different flavor of agua fresca ("fresh water"), the local soft drink. All kinds of fruit are used, as well as cucumber, spinach, carrots, and even grains and milk (see Horchata, page 36). Mixed with water and sugar, each of the various tantalizing combinations results in a refreshing beverage.

I was lucky to grow up just one exit from the San Diego/Mexico border. Back in those days it was easy to cross over to Mexico, so in my teen years, I would skateboard there with my pals. The promise of a cold agua fresca when I got to Mexico kept me rolling on the rough pavement.

For this version, I chose cantaloupe for the gorgeous pastel color and delicate perfumed flavor that goes perfectly with whey. Try it with whatever fruit you have on hand, and don't forget to add a few garnishes to make the pitcher look even more inviting.

YIELD 4–6 servings

INGREDIENTS

- 4 cups whey
- 3 cups chopped ripe cantaloupe (1 large cantaloupe)
- ½ cup sugar
- 2 cups water, optional
- Cantaloupe slices, mint leaves, and/or cucumber rounds for garnish
- Ice for serving

WHICH WHEY?
BEST Cooked, sweet
GOOD Acid

1 Combine the whey, cantaloupe, and sugar in a blender and blend until almost smooth. Leave some pulp to add to the fresh flavor. (If you're using a small blender, combine the ingredients in a bowl and blend the mixture in batches.)

2 Pour the mixture into a pitcher. Add more sweetener as desired. If you prefer a thinner drink, add up to 2 cups water.

3 Float garnishes in the pitcher or decorate individual glasses as desired. Serve over plenty of ice.

Store in the refrigerator and drink within 4 days.

Horchata
(Mexican Rice and Cinnamon Drink)

My absolute favorite agua fresca is agua de arroz, also known as horchata (the *h* is silent!). This light, cinnamon-rich rice milk is unbelievably good served ice cold. The horchata found in many Mexican restaurants in the US is too often made from a powdered mix—the homemade version is a completely different drink! This batch is large enough for sharing, or you can try the horchatte and the utterly delicious rumchata variations. Careful with rumchata, it goes down easy!

YIELD 8 servings

INGREDIENTS

- 4 cups whey
- 1½ cups cooked white or brown rice, any variety
- ½ cup almond flour or almond meal*
- ½ cup sugar or agave syrup
- 1 large stick Mexican cinnamon or ½ teaspoon ground cinnamon
- Pinch sea salt
- 4–5 cups cold water
- Ice for serving

*Or substitute 1 cup whole or slivered almonds, soaked overnight and drained before using.

WHICH WHEY?
BEST Cooked, sweet
OKAY Acid

1 Combine the whey, rice, almond flour, sugar, cinnamon, and salt in a blender and process until smooth. Add 4 cups water.

2 Strain the mixture through a nut-milk bag or a double layer of fine-mesh cheesecloth to catch any rice and almond grit.

3 Pour the liquid into a pitcher. Add more water if you prefer it thinner and more sugar if you want a sweeter drink. Serve over ice.

Store in the refrigerator and drink within 4 days.

Variations

Horchatte

Simmer 1 cup horchata until hot and whisk to make it foamy. If you have a milk frothing device, that will work great. Pour into a large coffee mug. Add a shot of espresso or as much strong brewed coffee as you'd like. Yum! And it's equally delicious cooled and poured over ice.

Rumchata

Mix 4 ounces horchata with 1 ounce white rum and stir. Serve with plenty of ice and enjoy!

What Is Mexican Cinnamon?

True cinnamon (*Cinnamomum verum*)—also called canela, Mexican cinnamon, or Ceylon cinnamon—is readily available in Mexican markets or online. Cassia (*C. cassia*) is more commonly found in the United States, but true cinnamon is ideal here because of its flaky, breakable texture in the blender and the traditional Mexican flavor it imparts. If you can only find cassia sticks, use ground cinnamon instead.

Strawberry Oat Milk

Oat milk is a popular and versatile alternative milk. Although it may be a new taste sensation for you or your family, I'm convinced that this tasty, bright version will convert even the most skeptical person. The addition of strawberries may recall a syrupy childhood drink, but the maple elevates the flavor. Using chilled whey and uncooked oats ensures that the resulting texture is pleasantly silky instead of viscous.

You can leave out the strawberries if you want to use this with your coffee for a frothy oat milk latte, but don't miss trying it with strawberries during their peak season for a real treat.

YIELD 4 servings

INGREDIENTS

- 4 cups whey, chilled
- 1 cup quick or rolled oats
- 1 cup fresh, hulled strawberries or thawed frozen strawberries
- ¼ cup maple syrup or sugar
- ½ teaspoon vanilla extract, optional
-    Pinch sea salt

WHICH WHEY?
BEST Cooked, sweet
GOOD Acid

1 Add the whey and oats to a blender and pulse for about 30 seconds to combine.

2 Add the strawberries, maple syrup, vanilla (if using), and salt, and blend just until smooth. If desired, strain the mixture through a nut-milk bag or a double layer of fine-mesh cheesecloth to filter out any oat grit and strawberry seeds.

3 Add more whey (or water) if you prefer a thinner drink and add more sweetener, if desired.

Store in the refrigerator and use within 4 days.

Sweet Almond Milk

Almonds have a nice flavor that works well with whey to create a delicious, versatile almond milk. Use it in smoothies and coffee drinks or to cook pudding or oatmeal, or just pour it over your favorite cereal. My trick of using almond flour makes it especially easy to whip up a batch.

YIELD 4 servings

INGREDIENTS

- 4 cups whey
- 1 cup almond flour or almond meal
- ¼ cup honey or 4 pitted dates
- Pinch sea salt

WHICH WHEY?
BEST Cooked, sweet
OKAY Acid

1 Blend the whey, almond flour, honey, and salt until smooth.

2 Strain the mixture through a nut-milk bag or a double layer of fine-mesh cheesecloth to filter out any grit.

3 Taste the almond milk. Add more whey (or water) if you prefer it thinner and more sweetener if you would like it sweeter.

Store in the refrigerator and use within 5 days.

Variation

Add ¼ cup unsweetened cocoa powder while blending for a yummy chocolate version.

Live Orange Soda

This delicious drink is fun to make. The fermentation process takes a few days, and monitoring its progress every day as the ferment turns into fizzy orange soda makes for a rewarding project! The rate of fermentation will depend on the temperature of your kitchen and how active your cultured acid whey (from yogurt or kefir) is.

If you are new to beverage fermentation, I highly recommend using a plastic bottle with a balloon over the opening instead of any kind of glass bottle with a lid. A clear plastic bottle and balloon allow you to safely monitor fermentation and carbonation as gas rises into the balloon. Sealed glass bottles can explode under pressure, so please use them only if you are experienced with fermenting beverages that create carbon dioxide.

YIELD 4 servings ••• **TIME** 4–7 days, 15 minutes active

INGREDIENTS

- 1 cup acid whey
- 2 cups freshly squeezed orange juice
- 2 cups water
- 3 tablespoons sugar

> **WHICH WHEY?**
> **BEST** Acid
> **NO WAY** Sweet, cooked

SPECIAL EQUIPMENT

- 2-liter clear plastic bottle
- Small balloon (or airlock)

1 Wash the bottle with hot, soapy water and rinse thoroughly to remove all residue of soap.

2 If curds are visible in the whey, strain it through a double layer of fine-mesh cheesecloth.

3 Pour the whey, orange juice, water, and sugar into the bottle. Stir or shake to dissolve the sugar. Cover the neck of the bottle with the balloon, making sure it is fastened securely.

4 Set the bottle in an undisturbed location to ferment. You want a spot where the temperature will stay between 72 and 78°F (22 and 25°C), if possible. The warmer the room, the faster fermentation will occur. It can take up to 6 days in my kitchen in chilly Portland, Oregon.

5 Allow the bacteria in the whey to eat the sugar for at least 24 hours so your soda isn't too sweet. Look for signs of fermentation: fizz and/or froth in the bottle, carbon dioxide filling the balloon, and maybe even a thin white film of harmless yeast

STEP 3:
Balloon fastened
to bottle

STEP 5:
Signs of
fermentation

that can appear as a natural part of the fermentation process. If the juice looks frothy and the balloon pops up within just a few hours, "burp" the bottle by lifting an edge of the balloon to release the carbon dioxide and replacing it around the neck of the bottle.

6 When you see clear signs of fermentation, remove the balloon, cap the bottle, and put it in the refrigerator to slow down fermentation. Chill for 24 hours before enjoying the orangey bubbles.

Store in the refrigerator and drink within 3 days. Feel the bottle daily, and if it is very firm, release carbonation by opening and reclosing the lid. Otherwise the soda might overflow like champagne when you open the bottle.

"Medicinal" Blueberry-Lavender Fizz

Many of the mass-marketed sodas we know today started as medicines in the nineteenth century. A mild fizz created by mixing baking soda and citric acid (the ingredients in many modern antacids) was supposed to help everything from indigestion to sluggishness to brain disorders. Today sugar and caffeine add kicks to our carbonated beverages, but that's nothing compared to the cocaine you might have encountered in some concoctions from a traveling medicine show!

This combination of good-for-you blueberries, tart lemon, soothing lavender, and creamy whey tastes much better than any medicinal brew or commercial soda. Feel free to act like an old-timey apothecary and mash up different combinations of fruit, herbs, and whole spices.

YIELD 4 servings

INGREDIENTS

- ½ cup blueberries, fresh or frozen and thawed
- Juice of 2 lemons
- 1 small sprig fresh lavender or ¼ teaspoon dried lavender flowers
- 4 tablespoons sugar or honey
- 1 teaspoon citric acid
- 3½ cups whey, chilled
- 1 teaspoon baking soda

WHICH WHEY?
BEST Cooked
GOOD Acid, sweet

SPECIAL EQUIPMENT

- 1-liter plastic (not glass) bottle with lid
- Funnel

1. Mash the blueberries with the lemon juice, lavender, sugar, and citric acid in a pitcher or large widemouthed jar. (Don't add the baking soda yet!)

2. Add the whey and stir to dissolve the sugar and citric acid. You can strain it for a clear soda, but I think the floating fruit and herbs add to the medicinal look. Pour the mixture into the bottle through a funnel, leaving 2 inches of room at the top. Wipe the funnel clean and put the lid nearby.

3. Add the baking soda to the bottle through the funnel and very quickly close the lid before the eruption of bubbles escapes. Once the initial foaming subsides, enjoy the drink immediately to experience the fizz, which will soon dissipate.

For a fun group activity, hold back the baking soda and pour the beverage into four individual cups. Let everyone add ¼ teaspoon baking soda to their own serving. Enjoy the collective squeal when the soda froths up!

Carbonated Whey?

If you have a soda machine that uses carbon dioxide canisters to make seltzer by the bottle, you can carbonate whey. Weird? Oh yeah! Awesome? Definitely.

Before carbonating cooked whey or acid whey, strain it through a double layer of fine-mesh cheesecloth to remove all solids. Carbonate the whey as you would water, and add flavor afterward, either to the bottle or by the glassful.

Carbonated whey is fun to play with! You can really let your imagination go wild with flavors. I like to add two herbal tea bags to one liter—simple but so flavorful and effective. Steep for 15 minutes to an hour, depending on how much flavor you want to impart.

For a savory soda in the style of a Persian *doogh*, make this recipe with yogurt whey. To serve, muddle a slice of cucumber in your glass, and add a sprinkle of dried mint and a pinch of salt to your drink.

Gianaclis's Fermented Strawberry-Mint Kefir

Gianaclis Caldwell is a fellow cheesemaker and author. I had the pleasure of taking one of her weekend cheesemaking courses on her family's homestead and dairy, Pholia Farm, in southern Oregon. The striking olive oil and paprika rinds she created on her large wheels of aged goat cheese made them look like ancient stones, and the sharp white cheese inside was incredible! She's also a master with other dairy delicacies. This recipe is adapted from her book *Homemade Yogurt & Kefir*.

YIELD 4 servings ••• **TIME** 24–48 hours, 10 minutes active

INGREDIENTS

- 4 cups whey
- 1 tablespoon kefir grains, rinsed
- ¼ cup fresh strawberries, hulled and sliced
- Mint leaves for serving

WHICH WHEY?
BEST Sweet, acid
GOOD Cooked

1 In a quart jar combine the whey, kefir grains, and strawberries. Cover lightly and let sit at room temperature for 24 to 48 hours.

2 Strain out the kefir grains and transfer to another container for future use.* Pick out the strawberry slices and return them to the whey kefir. Chill in the refrigerator for at least 3 hours before enjoying.

3 To serve, muddle a mint leaf at the bottom of a glass and pour the whey kefir on top. The strawberry slices can be strained out or left in.

Store in the refrigerator for up to a week (during this time a bit more fermentation will take place).

*To use the grains again, rinse them in cool nonchlorinated water and place in milk. (See page 20.)

You Can Culture Cooked Whey!

Though cooked whey from ricotta and other high-heat cheeses is the least nutritious whey option, you can liven it up with probiotics. Gianaclis notes in her book that research has shown kefir made from whey "has a similar final microbe profile, and probiotic potential, to kefir made with milk." Isn't that cool?

So if you want to turn your cooked (or sweet) whey into acid whey and give yourself a nice probiotic boost, you can do this with kefir grains.

Add a tablespoon of kefir grains to a quart of fully cooled cooked whey or sweet whey. Cover and leave for 12 to 24 hours. You can add a sugar source such as fruit, as Gianaclis does with strawberries, or a tablespoon of maple syrup, but it isn't necessary. There is sufficient lactose in the whey to ferment without added sugar.

After 12 hours, the whey kefir should taste tangy, and it might feel slightly effervescent on your tongue. It's alive! If you would like it a bit more fermented, leave it for a full 24 hours.

Now you can blend it with some fruit or simply drink a daily shot as is. Enjoy within 2 weeks.

Cocktails

Since whey contains electrolytes and vitamins, is it possible that it can combat a hangover when paired with alcohol? I like to think it can't hurt to infuse our cocktails with a little shot of probiotics. Well, even if that's wishful thinking, whey can do a lot for cocktails. It smooths tannins and mellows the taste of alcohol, removes bitterness, and adds texture. In some of these drinks, whey takes the place of milk in a pleasing way, and in others it acts like an emulsifying egg white to create froth.

Nicole's Lemon Meringue Pie Cocktail

Nicole Easterday owns and operates FARMcurious, where she teaches cheesemaking and fermenting classes. As an American Cheese Society Certified Cheese Professional and ACS Subject Matter Expert, she is a skilled cheesemaker *and* cheese monger! She can make a mean cheese board and tell you all kinds of fascinating history and science facts about each cheese.

Here she creatively takes some whey off our hands in this playful cocktail, which she developed using sweet whey from a cow's milk cheese. If you are making a pitcher, you can premix the ingredients, then shake each serving. Better yet, give each guest their own mason jar and let them prepare their own drinks.

YIELD 1 cocktail

INGREDIENTS

- ¼ cup finely crushed graham cracker crumbs
- Lemon slices
- 2 ounces cow's milk whey
- 2 ounces limoncello
- ½–1 ounce simple syrup (see recipe at right)
- ½ cup ice

WHICH WHEY?
BEST Any type

1 Spread the graham cracker crumbs on a plate. Moisten the rim of a glass with a lemon slice and dip the glass into the crumbs to coat the edge.

2 Add the whey, limoncello, and ½ ounce simple syrup to a cocktail shaker or mason jar. Add ice and shake to chill. Taste and add more simple syrup if desired.

3 Serve in the prepared glass, garnished with a lemon slice.

To make simple syrup, bring 1 cup water and 1 cup sugar to a boil. Stir to dissolve the sugar and let cool. Pour into a bottle to store. It will keep in the refrigerator for several months.

Summer Sipper

This whey-based version of a mint julep is a great cocktail to mix up in a pitcher for a cookout. It is lower in alcohol than a typical julep but just as welcome on a hot day—you can even increase the amount of whey or reduce the amount of bourbon for a refreshing summer cocktail to sip the whole afternoon.

YIELD 1 cocktail

INGREDIENTS

- 6 mint leaves
- 2 ounces whey
- 1½ ounces bourbon
- ½ ounce simple syrup (opposite)
- Crushed ice
- 2 cucumber slices for garnish

WHICH WHEY?
BEST Any type

1 Put the mint in a cocktail shaker or mason jar and crush the leaves lightly with a muddler or wooden spoon. Add the whey, bourbon, simple syrup, and ice, and shake well.

2 Strain into a glass, pouring the drink over more crushed ice if desired. Garnish with the cucumber slices.

Lightweight Caipirinha

A caipirinha, the popular Brazilian cocktail, is delicious, but it's basically a large shot of flavored hard liquor. If I drank a couple of these made in the traditional way, I'd need a nap and my day would be over. Instead, I simply use the potent liquor to spike a tall glass of Brazilian Limeade. That gives me a larger cocktail with less alcohol but all the great flavor. For entertaining, you can make up a pitcher (minus the ice) ahead of time and pour over ice right before serving.

This caipirinha does taste a little different from the original, but the cachaça and lime along with the mellowing whey make it a delicious cocktail I'm sure any Brazilian would appreciate.

YIELD 1 cocktail

INGREDIENTS

Ice

4 ounces Brazilian Limeade (page 31)

1 ounce cachaça or light rum

Lime wedge for garnish

WHICH WHEY?
BEST Any type

Fill a glass with ice and add the limeade, then stir in the cachaça. Garnish with a lime wedge.

Cachaça, pronounced ka-cha-suh, is a sugarcane-based spirit. If you can't find it, use rum.

Hannah's Jamaica Rum Punch

Kombucha Mamma Hannah Crum is the founder of Kombucha Kamp and coauthor of *The Big Book of Kombucha*. The *Jamaica* in the recipe name refers to what has come to be known as the Mexican hibiscus flower (not the tropical island of Jamaica) and is pronounced Ha-MAY-ca in Spanish. Knowing that Hannah's love of Mexico, probiotics, and tart flavors runs deep, I wasn't surprised at all when I saw this recipe.

The first step is making a tart herbal tea. If you use whey to make the tea, any small curds will bond with tannins in the spices and flowers. When the tea is strained, any bitter elements are removed, leaving a smooth, tasty mixture. The additional whey in the punch adds to a luscious mouthfeel in this cocktail. Hannah formulated this recipe using acid whey from milk kefir.

YIELD 18–20 servings ••• **TIME** 1 hour, 10 minutes active

JAMAICA TEA

- ½ cup dried hibiscus flowers or 8 hibiscus tea bags
- 1 tablespoon chai spice blend (see note)
- 1 cinnamon stick
- 4 cups whey or water
- ½ cup sugar

PUNCH

- 1 (750 ml) bottle white rum
- 4 cups jamaica tea
- 4 cups berry- or ginger-flavored kombucha
- 2 cups whey
- 2 tablespoons triple sec
- Juice of one lime

FOR SERVING

Ice

Orange slices or lime wedges

WHICH WHEY?
BEST Sweet, acid
OKAY Cooked

1 **MAKE THE JAMAICA TEA.** Add the hibiscus, chai spice, and cinnamon stick to a pot with the whey.

2 Bring to a boil over high heat. Reduce the heat and simmer for 20 minutes. Stir in the sugar to dissolve. Strain thoroughly. Allow to cool.

3 **MAKE THE PUNCH.** In a large pitcher or punch bowl, combine the rum, cooled jamaica tea, kombucha, whey, triple sec, and lime juice, and stir to blend.

Serve over ice with an orange slice or lime wedge garnish. Refrigerate any leftovers and drink within 4 days.

If you don't have chai spice, make your own blend with equal parts allspice, cloves, nutmeg, ginger, and dried orange peel.

Whey and Honey Cocktail

This comforting cocktail is at once festive and humble. The flavor and golden color of the honey-flavored liqueur Benedictine are natural complements to the milky whey. In addition to sweetness, Benedictine offers complex botanical flavors (from 27 spices, herbs, and peels) that make this cocktail truly special. A simple honey liqueur that you make yourself (see Homemade Spiced Honey Liqueur, opposite) will also work well. Hot or cold, this drink is like a sweet hug.

YIELD 1 cocktail

INGREDIENTS

- 6 ounces whey
- 1 ounce Benedictine or Homemade Spiced Honey Liqueur (opposite)
- 1 orange slice, optional

WHICH WHEY?
BEST Sweet, cooked
OKAY Acid

COLD VERSION. Refrigerate the whey until very cold. Pour the Benedictine into a clear glass, add a couple of ice cubes, top with the chilled whey, and stir. Garnish with a slice of orange, if you like.

HOT VERSION. Warm the whey over low heat. Pour the Benedictine into a mug and strain the hot whey over it. Garnish with a slice of orange, if you like.

This cocktail traditionally contains milk, so if you would like more viscosity, add a splash of milk, half-and-half, or cream. I like using my milk frother, with cold or hot milk, and topping the cocktail with a little milk foam and ground cinnamon.

HOMEMADE SPICED HONEY LIQUEUR

YIELD 1 cup ••• **TIME** 2–24 hours, a few minutes active

- ⅔ cup whiskey
- ⅓ cup honey
- 2-inch piece lemon peel
- 2-inch piece orange peel
- 1-inch sprig rosemary
- 1 star anise pod
- 1 cinnamon stick
- 1 whole clove

1 In a measuring cup, combine the whiskey and honey and stir thoroughly until the honey is dissolved.

2 Gently crush together the lemon peel, orange peel, rosemary, star anise, cinnamon stick, and clove in a 1-pint jar. Pour the honey and whiskey mix into the jar, and allow the mixture to infuse for at least 2 but preferably up to 24 hours.

3 Strain into a clean glass bottle or jar.

The liqueur will keep at room temperature indefinitely.

Espresso Martini

This cocktail is a nice double whammy for either a Sunday-morning brunch or an energizing pick-me-up before a night on the town (you maniac!). The method for making a whey-based, espresso-infused simple syrup is easy, though it takes a few minutes of forethought. The benefit of boiling the whey is that any tiny curds that appear will attract tannins from the espresso grounds, giving a mellow coffee flavor without bitterness. The resulting cocktail brings to mind a spiked and ultra-smooth cold brew coffee and is almost too delicious—drink with caution!

YIELD 1 cocktail • • • **TIME** 35 minutes, 5 minutes active

FOR THE ESPRESSO SIMPLE SYRUP

- 1 cup sugar
- 1 cup whey
- 3 tablespoons ground espresso

FOR THE COCKTAIL

- 2 ounces vodka
- 1 ounce espresso, freshly brewed, or unsweetened cold brew
- ½ ounce espresso simple syrup
- Ice

WHICH WHEY?
BEST Sweet, cooked
OKAY Acid

1 **MAKE THE ESPRESSO SIMPLE SYRUP.** Bring the sugar, whey, and ground espresso to a boil in a small pot. Remove from the heat and allow to steep for 10 minutes. Strain through a double layer of fine-mesh cheesecloth and cool.

2 **MAKE THE COCKTAIL.** Combine the vodka, espresso, and espresso simple syrup in a shaker or mason jar. Add ice and shake until frothy. Strain into a martini glass.

The espresso simple syrup will keep in the refrigerator for up to 5 days.

If you are making drinks for a crowd, you can premix the ingredients then shake each serving for that great froth. Better yet, give each guest their own mason jar and let them do their own shaking and pouring into their serving glass. It makes for a fun brunch activity.

Wheyward Sour

You've heard of using egg whites or, more recently, aquafaba (liquid from chickpeas) for shaken cocktails, right? You'll be happy to know that whey creates that same rich froth when shaken. Emily Darchuk and I collaborated to create a Wheyward Sour featuring her Wheyward Spirit. Tangy acid whey (from yogurt) and lemon juice complement her waste-free spirit perfectly, but any whey will froth up nicely in this unique cocktail. Support a sustainable, woman-owned business while enjoying a real treat. Cheers to that!

YIELD 1 cocktail

INGREDIENTS

- 2 ounces Wheyward Spirit (see Distilling Whey, page 56)
- ½ ounce acid whey
- ½ ounce freshly squeezed lemon juice
- ½ ounce simple syrup (see page 48)
- Ice
- Angostura bitters
- Lemon peel for garnish

WHICH WHEY?
BEST Acid
GOOD Sweet
OKAY Cooked

1 Add the Wheyward Spirit, whey, lemon juice, and simple syrup to a shaker or mason jar with a lid. Shake vigorously until emulsified. Add ice and shake again until you see foam and the cocktail is ice cold.

2 Strain into a coupe glass and top with a shake of Angostura bitters and the lemon peel.

Distilling Whey

In addition to making cocktails with whey, you can distill whey into a high-proof spirit. This traditional craft has been practiced in diverse places ranging from yurts in Mongolia to the first whey-to-ethanol plant in Ireland in 1978 to a company called Wheyward Spirit in Portland, Oregon.

Wheyward Spirit founder and CEO Emily Darchuk began her career as a food scientist in the natural foods and dairy industries. Observing how the problem of whey waste impacts small communities motivated her to do something about it. As a scientist, she knew she could convert whey into alcohol. However, as a consumer who cares about the impact of her purchases, she wanted to make something unique for others who, like her, care about the origin of their food.

She launched Wheyward Spirit in 2020, after perfecting this unique spirit through hundreds of hours of trials, carefully crafting the recipe while she mastered the distillation process. This smooth, impressive base spirit, which can be used in place of vodka, gin, or rum, was named a Good Foods Award winner in a blind tasting against regular vodkas.

When Emily hosted me for a private tasting, she presented Wheyward Spirit on the rocks, then in two heavenly cocktails. The addition of lemon juice and zest was especially tasty, making me think of lemon curd. This combination inspired the Wheyward Sour (page 55) that Emily and I created.

Wheyward Spirit retains some of the whey's body and silkiness without coming across as a dairy-based liquor. Having experimented a bit with producing alcohol from fermented whey (see page 58), I'm especially impressed that her result retains just enough whey characteristics to allow for a clean and refreshing mouthfeel. Emily says the secret is making it taste good at all stages, otherwise it's garbage in, garbage out. To think that some people consider whey a waste product!

I can't wait to see where Emily takes this next. You can order and find more unique cocktail recipes at www.wheywardspirit.com.

Sparkling Honey Wine

When I learned about airag, a traditional Mongolian low-alcohol beverage that makes it easier to digest high-lactose mare's milk, and arki, the distilled version that is akin to vodka, I was intrigued. Further research turned up a sparkling dairy beverage called blaand with purported Viking roots that was likely made with cultured buttermilk. Inspired, I decided to dive into whey-based hooch making!

Something between wine and mead, my creation is wonderfully effervescent, full bodied, sweet, and quite boozy! I used a hydrometer to measure the alcohol, which came in at 5 percent right before refrigeration.

I like adding the flavors in the second, refrigerated (slower) fermentation and after the yeast has already taken hold. That way, nothing gets in the way of the primary fermentation. Adding rosemary gives the ferment a strong herbal flavor that balances the sweetness. Cracked coffee or cacao beans add a nice bitterness that goes well with the milky, stoutlike mouthfeel of the wine.

It will be quite sweet if you drink it within the first two weeks. It does get drier the more it ferments under refrigeration. Since you have to "burp" the bottles daily, it is worth tasting it throughout the weeks. You can also dilute the wine by half with seltzer water or add it to cocktails to temper its sweetness.

YIELD 2 quarts ••• **TIME** 2 weeks minimum, 30 minutes active

INGREDIENTS

- 6 cups whey (about what is left from a half-gallon-of-milk batch of cheese)
- 1¾ cups raw honey (any honey will work, but raw honey ferments more easily)
- ½ teaspoon champagne yeast or other wine yeast

Optional flavorings to be added in the second fermentation:

- 1 sprig rosemary
- 2 sprigs lemon thyme
- 2 pieces lemon zest
- 2 teaspoons cracked coffee beans
- 2 teaspoons cacao nibs or cracked cacao beans

WHICH WHEY?
BEST Cooked
GOOD Sweet
NO WAY Acid

SANITIZING YOUR EQUIPMENT

Before making any ferment, your equipment must be completely clean so as not to contaminate the process. You can use a sanitizers like Star San or iodophor, which are no-rinse, no-chlorine sanitizers used by brewers for glass and plastic. For glass, washing with soap and hot water works well. I like to give the bottles a final rinse with plain boiled water also. Allow the bottles to cool completely. Do not use bleach—it breaks down plastic and can impede fermentation if not rinsed extremely well.

SPECIAL EQUIPMENT

Choose one of these options for a safe fermenting vessel.

- Two 1-liter plastic bottles fitted with airlocks or rubber balloons
- A half-gallon glass jug fitted with an airlock or rubber balloon
- A half-gallon glass canning jar with a lid fitted with an airlock or rubber balloon

SAFETY NOTE: I try to avoid using plastic but this is a very active ferment. If your home is warmer than 72°F (22°C) and you will not be able to release carbonation *daily* throughout the entire process, including refrigeration, I recommend that you use plastic bottles with airlocks or balloons from start to finish. This is a fun experiment, but please be safe, as sugar and yeast can cause glass bottles to explode.

1 Sanitize all equipment that will come in contact with the whey, honey, or yeast (see Sanitizing Your Equipment, above).

2 No matter what type of whey you're using, clarify it first by boiling and straining to remove as many solids as possible. Let the whey cool completely at room temperature (cover to avoid gathering wild yeasts).

3 Stir the honey into the whey until it dissolves. Taste the mixture now so you can recognize the difference when it turns into wine. Use a clean spoon and do not double-dip!

4 Pour the sweetened whey into the fermenting bottle or bottles using a funnel. Leave at least 3 inches of space at the top for foam to build up.

continued on next page

5 Sprinkle the yeast over the top of the whey and allow it to hydrate for 5 minutes. Stir to combine.

6 Cover the fermenting vessels with airlocks or balloons—do not seal them with a conventional lid. Keep in mind that even plastic bottle lids can pop off and hurt you as you unscrew them if too much carbon dioxide has built up.

7 Leave the magical mixture to do its work. Fermentation will occur more quickly in a warm place (e.g., a 72°F/22°C kitchen) than in a cool one (e.g., a 55°F/13°C basement). If your environment is warm, you may see bubbling in the airlocks within 24 to 48 hours, the balloons will inflate, and/or foam will appear inside the bottles. The yeast is feasting on the sugar. It's very exciting!

8 Monitor the bottles daily. Once you see the signs of fermentation described above, allow the fermentation to continue at room temperature for 7 days. Make sure active bubbling and foaming have stopped before moving on. Move the bottles to a cooler area if the ferment is more active than you'd like or if you're going away for a day or two. If a balloon gets very taut, release the pressure by removing the balloon, letting the carbon dioxide out, and replacing the balloon on the bottle.

9 Unless the mixture smells bad or you see mold growth, taste it. It should taste boozy and warm your belly. If you have a hydrometer, you can use it now to check the alcohol content. Add any optional flavorings, if desired. If you'd like to use two different flavorings, use half the recommended amount of each in a bottle. Measurements given are each for a half gallon.

10 Transfer the bottles to the refrigerator. If you're using glass, keep the airlocks or balloons in place. If you're using plastic bottles, you can replace the airlocks or balloons with screw-on lids but only if you can check the bottles daily and release gas, a.k.a. "burping" the bottles. I like using plastic bottles because you can tell if they need burping by checking the firmness.

11 Start tasting the wine after 2 full days (48 hours). If you're happy with the taste, you can remove the flavorings, or if you prefer a stronger flavor, leave them in. Rosemary is strong and will flavor the wine quickly; other flavorings may take longer. You can

drink your honey wine now. Put the airlock or balloon back on the bottle if you have any leftover wine.

12 Continue to monitor and burp the bottles daily. The wine will clarify a bit under refrigeration. Solids will settle at the bottom of the bottles, and the top portion will still be honey colored but not as cloudy. If you prefer a cleaner appearance, you can carefully pour the clear portion into fresh bottles, using a sieve to remove the dregs. If you don't see any fermentation activity after 2 weeks, you can replace the airlocks or balloons with lids. Continue to monitor and burp the bottles daily for another week.

That's it! The fizz will eventually go away but the honey wine will still be delicious. It will get less sweet the longer you leave the yeast to eat the sugar. Store in the refrigerator and enjoy within 3 weeks for best flavor. When opening, always point bottles away from yourself and others and hold a towel over the lid. Pretend it's a bottle of champagne and celebrate your whey wine!

Fermenting Whey into Biofuel

We've now seen that whey can turn juice into a fizzy soda, kefir grains can culture cooked whey, and honey and whey can make sparkling wine, all via the power of fermentation. Perhaps now it will seem more feasible that whey can turn into a fuel. That's right, scientists around the world have been working on this for decades. There are challenges just like with any alternative fuel, but the research is alive and well. Can you imagine a day when you can say your car is whey powered?!

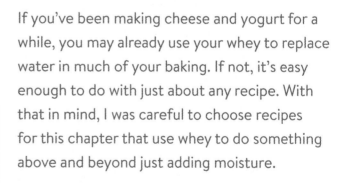

Bread

If you've been making cheese and yogurt for a while, you may already use your whey to replace water in much of your baking. If not, it's easy enough to do with just about any recipe. With that in mind, I was careful to choose recipes for this chapter that use whey to do something above and beyond just adding moisture.

In baked goods, the natural sugar in whey promotes great browning in a crust, and the flavor adds a mild cheesiness or tang. In addition to benefiting from these characteristics of whey, these recipes are all very easy to make, too!

No-Knead Ciabatta

Ciabatta, which means "slipper" in Italian, refers to the similarity of this loaf's long, flat shape to that of a slip-on indoor shoe. This recipe's no-knead method, popularized by Jim Lahey, makes this bread perfect for a lazy (or busy) baker. That's me, cozily "loafing" around in my slippers making bread. This is the only bread in the book that uses yeast, but it's as easy as bread baking gets. The recipe produces a wet dough that uses moisture, time, and just a pinch of yeast to create a soft, bubbly texture. Baking it in a covered pot creates a great crust.

This is the classic ciabatta, but you can easily add fresh rosemary and olives or dried cranberries, chocolate chunks, and orange zest to create special loaves worthy of gift giving. This bread is best eaten fresh. The next day it's still tasty when toasted, and it can go into Gazpacho (page 78) on the third day.

YIELD 2 small loaves ⋯ **TIME** 20 hours, 20 minutes active

INGREDIENTS

- 3 cups all-purpose or bread flour, plus more for dusting
- 1¼ teaspoons sea salt
- ¼ teaspoon instant or other active bread yeast
- 1½ cups whey

WHICH WHEY?
BEST Sweet
GOOD Cooked, acid

SPECIAL EQUIPMENT

Choose one of these special options for baking.

- 2 large cast-iron pots with lids or other oven-safe pots or pans with domed lids that will not touch the bread as it rises
- 2 baking sheets or pizza stones and 2 oven-safe pans to use as lids

NOTE: Thoroughly clean all baking equipment to remove oil and other residue that might smoke during high-heat baking.

1 Whisk the flour, salt, and yeast in a large bowl. Add the whey and mix with a wooden spoon just until everything is incorporated. The dough will be wet and sticky.

2 Cover the bowl with a clean tea towel and let it sit at room temperature until the dough has more than doubled in size and the surface looks bubbly, 12 to 18 hours.

3 Dust the dough with flour in the bowl and with floured hands, a scraper, or a wooden spoon, stretch and fold the dough over itself one way and then the other way to make a neat square that fits snugly in the bowl again. (You can do this on a floured work surface if you prefer, but I don't like the extra mess.)

4 Cover the bowl and allow the dough to rise for another hour or until doubled in size. It should keep an indent when you poke it with your finger. If it immediately springs back, let it rise for 20 minutes longer.

5 While the dough rises, place the cast-iron pots (without lids) or baking sheets in the oven and preheat the oven to 475°F (245°C).

6 Cut the dough into two equal pieces and flour both pieces generously on all sides. I repeat, generously.

7 Take one pot or baking sheet out of the oven and set it on a heatproof surface. Dust it with flour.

8 Stretch one piece of dough into a rectangle that will fit under the lid, and transfer it to the pot. Cover the pot and put it in the oven. Repeat with the other loaf. Bake for 20 minutes.

9 Remove the lids and bake, uncovered, for 20 minutes longer. The crust should be the color of a walnut shell. However, it is nice when the bottom gets a little darker, more like a hazelnut shell. When you knock lightly on the loaf with your knuckles, it should feel hard and sound hollow.

10 Let the loaves cool completely on a rack. I know it's hard to wait, but this is an important step, as residual heat continues to cook the bread as it cools. If you slice into it too early, it will be gummy. While it cools, listen to the crackling sounds the crust makes. That's a bread song!

This bread is best eaten within 2 days. After the third day, use it to make croutons or to thicken gazpacho and other soups. The bread can also be frozen for up to 6 months.

Skillet Cornbread

Cornbread is so easy to make that I always wonder why I don't prepare it more often. It helps make a simple meal special and hearty without spending hours in the kitchen. Just mix it up and pop it in the oven, and by the time the rest of your meal is scraped together and on the table, toasty cornbread is ready to serve. Whey gives it a richness that's just perfect with butter and honey.

YIELD 8 servings ••• **TIME** 45 minutes, 10 minutes active

INGREDIENTS

- ¼ cup salted butter
- 1½ cups whey
- 1 cup cornmeal (not too fine)
- 1 cup self-rising flour*
- 2 eggs
- ½ cup corn kernels, fresh or frozen and thawed
- 2 tablespoons honey
- ¼ teaspoon fine salt
- 2 tablespoons fresh or pickled jalapeños, diced (optional)

*Or 1 cup all-purpose flour plus 2 teaspoons baking powder and an extra pinch of salt

WHICH WHEY?
BEST Any type

1. Preheat the oven to 400°F (200°C). As the oven warms, put the butter in a cast-iron skillet, and put the skillet in the oven until the butter melts. (Don't forget it's in there!)

2. Combine the whey, cornmeal, flour, eggs, corn, honey, salt, and jalapeños, if using, in a large bowl. Pour the melted butter into the bowl, leaving a generous coating in the skillet. Stir until well combined and pour the mixture into the buttered skillet.

3. Bake for 25 minutes, or until a toothpick comes out clean and the top is just golden and the edges are a little toasty. Allow to cool for 10 minutes and dig in.

Eat or freeze within 3 days.

Heather's Flatbread

Among her many talents, Heather Arndt Anderson is a botanist, food historian, writer, and teacher. I was lucky to have her help testing recipes for my book *Instant Pot Cheese*, and because she is not one to waste food, she ended up with a freezer full of whey. When her drool-inducing photos of flatbreads and other creations made with her whey started appearing on social media, I knew I had to get her recipe. As expected, this versatile flatbread is perfectly crusty, chewy, and quick to throw together to complete a meal. Heather developed this recipe using acid whey from cow's milk cheese.

YIELD 12 flatbreads ••• **TIME** 1 hour, 30 minutes active

INGREDIENTS

- 3 cups all-purpose flour, plus more for dusting
- 1 tablespoon kosher salt
- 1 tablespoon baking powder
- 1 cup whey
- 2 tablespoons olive oil
- 2 tablespoons sourdough starter (optional, but adds nice flavor)
- Ghee or oil for cooking
- Za'atar for finishing, optional

WHICH WHEY?
BEST Acid
GOOD Sweet, cooked

1 Combine the flour, salt, and baking powder in a large mixing bowl. Stir together the whey, olive oil, and sourdough starter in a separate bowl until well combined. Make a well in the center of the flour mixture and pour in the whey mixture, stirring together with a fork until a shaggy dough is formed.

2 Turn the dough out onto a floured surface and knead until the dough is soft and slightly elastic (it will be a bit tacky to the touch), 5 minutes. Cover the dough with an overturned mixing bowl and allow it to rest for 30 minutes.

3 Divide the dough into 12 portions and roll each into a ball. Heat a griddle or large skillet over medium heat, and brush it with a little ghee or oil.

4 Lightly oil your hands and work surface, then flatten each ball with your fingers and the heel of your hand until the dough is about ¼ inch thick. Cook the flatbreads until golden brown, about 2 minutes on each side.

5 After they come off the griddle, brush the flatbreads with extra ghee and add a sprinkle of kosher salt or za'atar.

Store in a bag or airtight container. Flatbreads will keep up to 5 days at room temperature or a month in the freezer. Reheat in the oven at 350°F (180°C) before serving.

No-Yeast Pizza Dough

There are times when you just need pizza *now*. Not delivery, not in a few hours after the dough rises—now! For those times, I am so glad to have this dough recipe at the ready. The trick is using yogurt whey and self-rising flour. The acid in the whey works with the baking powder in the flour to create a crispy and chewy pizza crust with no need for a long rise.

Pizza toppings I keep in my pantry, refrigerator, or freezer at any given time are hard cheeses, pepperoni, prosciutto, pesto, olives, and sun-dried tomatoes. Any vegetable and meat left from another meal makes a great option, too. You can even top your pizza with a bunch of arugula and a fried egg! There are no rules when it comes to toppings.

YIELD 2 large or 4 small pizzas ••• **TIME** 30 minutes

INGREDIENTS

- 2 cups self-rising flour, plus more for dusting
- 1 teaspoon sea salt
- 1 cup acid whey

  Olive oil

WHICH WHEY?
BEST Acid
OKAY Sweet, cooked

SPECIAL EQUIPMENT

- 2 cast-iron skillets or other oven-safe pans

1 Have all your toppings prepared and at hand. Preheat the oven to 400°F (200°C).

2 Measure the flour and salt into a bowl. Whisk to mix evenly. Pour all the whey in and stir to create the dough. If it's very wet, add more flour 1 tablespoon at a time until all the dough comes together into a ball. If it's a little sticky, that's fine.

3 Preheat both skillets on the stovetop over medium heat. Preheating the pans ensures a crispy crust. This is a no-soggy-pizza zone!

4 Cut the dough into two pieces.

5 Flour a cutting board liberally. Transfer one piece of dough onto the board and, with a floured rolling pin, roll it into a circle that will fit in the skillet (or whatever the shape of the pans you're using).

6   Lightly oil one skillet and slide the rolled-out dough into it. Cook on the stovetop until the bottom of the crust is golden brown, about 5 minutes. Add the toppings. Move the pan to the oven and bake for 7 to 10 minutes, or until any cheese is melted and the outer perimeter of the crust is browned on top.

7   While the first pizza cooks, roll out the second ball of dough and repeat. Transfer the pizzas to a cutting board, allow to cool slightly, and cut into slices to serve.

SUBSTITUTIONS

If you don't have self-rising flour or enough acid whey, don't despair. These substitutions work in a pinch, though the texture of the crust will change.

SELF-RISING FLOUR: Mix 2 cups all-purpose flour with 1 tablespoon baking powder and a big pinch of salt.

ACID WHEY: Add 2 teaspoons apple cider vinegar to 1 cup whey (any kind).

Pão de Queijo
(Brazilian Cheese Bread)

These crusty, chewy little bread rolls from Brazil would be love at first bite for any cheese lover anywhere in the world, I'm sure of it. As they are traditionally made with tapioca starch (also called tapioca flour), they make an especially great surprise for anyone avoiding gluten. This convenient blender-and-muffin-tin version doesn't exactly follow the traditional process, but the resulting flavor and dreamy texture are so close to the real thing that I see no reason for hand shaping the rolls. But don't even think of using cupcake liners, which ruin the mandatory crust on the rolls. I learned that the hard way!

The batter is so loose and liquid that it seems like it can't be right, but trust the whey—it will work. Once you try the basic recipe, you can change things up by adding bacon crumbles, diced jalapeño, chives, or any other bits you might enjoy in cheese rolls.

YIELD 36 rolls ••• **TIME** 25 minutes

INGREDIENTS

- 2   cups tapioca starch
- 1   cup whey
- 1   cup crumbled or shredded cheeses (see note) or 1 cup grated Parmesan cheese
- 2   eggs
- ½   cup olive oil
- 1   teaspoon sea salt

WHICH WHEY?
BEST Acid
GOOD Sweet, cooked

In the US it isn't easy to find the Brazilian Minas cheese or queijo meia cura traditionally used to make pão de queijo, so I re-create it as best I can. I use ½ cup crumbled cotija cheese (my Brazilian friend Rita confirmed that this is a good choice) and another ½ cup shredded sharp cheese, such as aged cheddar, but the recipe is flexible. You can even use mozzarella.

1 Preheat the oven to 350°F (180°C). Lightly oil or butter two muffin tins.

2 Add the tapioca starch, whey, cheese, eggs, oil, and salt to a blender and blend on low to medium speed until combined thoroughly. Try to avoid creating foam. Pour the batter all the way to the top of the muffin cups. We want a generous dome to form on the rolls as they rise. It's okay if they squeeze out of their cups as they bake.

3 Bake for 15 to 20 minutes. The rolls should rise and be light golden on top with a slightly darker crust on the bottom.

4 Let the rolls cool slightly before enjoying them. If you have any left over, store them wrapped at room temperature. Reheat for a few minutes before eating because they soften up.

Well wrapped, these rolls keep in the freezer for up to 3 months. To reheat, pop frozen rolls into a 400°F (200°C) oven for 5 minutes.

DONENESS DETAILS

If you have never had pão de queijo, you may wonder if they are raw when you note the chewy (some would say gummy) texture and the look of melted cheese inside. These characteristics, which are typical of tapioca starch, are what make this bread unique. After you take the rolls out of the oven, their insides will continue to cook a little more with residual heat.

Look for a light brown crust on the bottom and sides, and a barely golden color on the top. The inside shouldn't be runny or clearly uncooked, but it shouldn't be fluffy like a typical yeast roll either. The texture of warm but not fully melted cheese is a good gauge.

Savories

Whey can be a standout ingredient in soups, salads, and sides. Use it to soak beans, rice, and grains to make them easier to cook and digest while also imparting some extra flavor. It makes a great base for broth and can be used as a poaching liquid. The sweetness and richness of whey shines in risotto, pasta dishes, and cream sauces.

It also makes an excellent brining liquid, tenderizing tough cuts and helping marinades infuse meat with flavor.

Cream of Broccoli Soup

Cream-based soups can feel heavy and too rich, so I usually reserve them for winter holidays and cold weather. Using whey instead of milk or cream, I can create a silky texture without the heavy feeling in the gut and the need for a nap! Here we use tapioca starch and potatoes for texture. The combination allows us to cut out the cream entirely and reduce the cheese. Amazingly, it still tastes like a comforting cheesy soup!

Feel free to replace the broccoli with asparagus, winter squash, cauliflower, or another hearty vegetable. They all work beautifully.

YIELD 4 servings ••• **TIME** 40 minutes

INGREDIENTS

- ¼ cup ghee or olive oil
- 1 cup diced carrot
- ½ cup diced onion
- 2 cloves garlic, minced
- ¼ teaspoon paprika
- ¼ teaspoon black pepper
- ¼ teaspoon mustard powder or ½ teaspoon yellow mustard
- 2 tablespoons tapioca starch or all-purpose flour
- 4 cups whey
- 3 cups broccoli florets and chopped peeled stems
- 2 cups diced potatoes
- 1 teaspoon salt
- 1 cup shredded sharp cheddar cheese

  Croutons or crusty bread for serving

1 Warm 2 tablespoons of the ghee in a large pot over medium heat. Add the carrot and onion, and sauté until glossy and fragrant, about 5 minutes. Lower the heat to medium low.

2 Add the garlic, paprika, pepper, and mustard, and toast for a minute or two to bring out their flavors without burning them.

3 Add the remaining 2 tablespoons ghee and stir in the tapioca starch. It will sizzle and not thicken yet. Cook the starch in the oil, stirring, for 1 minute.

4 Whisk in the whey slowly. Add the broccoli, potatoes, and salt.

5 Cook the soup over low heat until the vegetables are fork-tender, 20 minutes. This is a great time to taste and season with more salt and pepper if needed.

WHICH WHEY?
BEST Sweet, cooked
OKAY Acid

6   If you have an immersion blender, you can blend the soup right in the pot. I leave about a quarter of the veggies in chunks for some bite, but the amount you blend is up to you.

   If you have a countertop blender, blend the soup in batches. Carefully ladle some of the soup into the blender. Be sure to fill it no more than halfway and to vent the lid to let steam escape. (A sealed container of hot soup can explode.) Blend until the soup is as smooth as you desire and then transfer to a large heat-resistant bowl. Repeat until all the soup is blended and then return the soup to the pot.

7   Simmer the soup for 5 minutes. Just before serving, add the cheddar a little at a time and stir to distribute. Serve with croutons made with leftover Ciabatta (page 64) or any crusty bread.

Refrigerate and enjoy within 5 days.

Don't Use Whey to Ferment Vegetables!

Having followed a recipe many years ago for fermenting carrots using whey and not liking the result at all, I was so glad to have my friend Kirsten Shockey, author of *Fermented Vegetables* and other books, clarify this issue for me.

There is a common belief that whey can (and should) be used for fermenting vegetables. This belief is likely based on the fact that both vegetables and dairy ferments utilize species of *Lactobacillus* bacteria. Adding whey to vegetables to help ferment them assumes two things—that the vegetables can't start a good ferment without added bacteria and that all forms of *Lactobacillus* are the same.

The truth is you simply don't need added starter for vegetables to ferment. Putting plant-eating bacteria in your cheese or putting cheese eaters in your sauerkraut just doesn't make sense. Dairy cultures don't help the bacteria that are already in the vegetable ferment. Adding them doesn't speed up the fermentation, and it often makes your vegetables a little mushy and cheesy tasting, neither of which is what you are looking for.

Butternut Corn Chowder

There are some comforts I have to embrace when the summer gardening season ends and dark and rainy months are around the corner: new ingredients to work with, warming spices, and all the hygge ("coziness") I can conjure. This chowder is all that in a bowl! It's a truly transitional dish, bringing the harvest of late summer and early fall into a new season. Whey adds a wonderful creaminess to all soups, but it works really well with the sweetness of corn and squash.

YIELD 4–8 servings ••• **TIME** 45 minutes

INGREDIENTS

- 3 tablespoons olive oil or ghee
- 2½ cups corn kernels, fresh or frozen
- 2 cups cubed butternut squash
- 1 cup diced onion
- ½ cup diced celery
- 1 clove garlic, crushed
- 2 teaspoons tandoori spice blend or garam masala
- 1½ teaspoons chili powder
- ½ teaspoon black pepper
- ¼ teaspoon white pepper
- ½ teaspoon sea salt
- 4 cups whey
- ¼ cup heavy cream, optional
- 1 tablespoon honey, optional

  Sour cream or crème fraîche for serving, optional

  Torn cilantro leaves for serving, optional

WHICH WHEY?
BEST Sweet, cooked
OKAY Acid

1 Heat the oil in a large pot over medium heat. Add the corn, squash, onion, and celery, and cook until the onion is soft, about 5 minutes.

2 Add the garlic, tandoori spice, chili powder, black pepper, and white pepper, and heat for just a minute or two—avoid burning the garlic or it will get bitter. Season with the salt.

3 Add the whey and simmer until the squash is tender, about 25 minutes.

4 For a creamy chowder, blend half of the soup in a blender (careful!) or use an immersion blender and leave the soup as chunky or smooth as you like. Taste and add more salt and pepper if needed. Stir in the heavy cream and honey, if using.

5 Serve with a dollop of sour cream, and top with cilantro, if you like.

Refrigerate leftover soup and eat within 5 days.

Gazpacho

I have to admit, when I first heard about gazpacho, I couldn't get past the idea that it would be like chugging a jar of marinara sauce. I couldn't have been more wrong! The secrets of this fresh tomato soup are the bread, juicy tomatoes in season, and plenty of olive oil. In experimenting with adding whey to the recipe, I was surprised that I was able to reduce the olive oil because whey adds light richness. Interestingly, I also found the whey-based soup more filling. Since this soup is never heated, you retain the probiotic goodness of acid whey, if that is what you use.

YIELD 4–8 servings • • • **TIME** 2½ hours, 30 minutes active

INGREDIENTS

- 2 thick slices of rustic white bread (see No-Knead Ciabatta, page 64); day-old bread is just fine
- 2 cups whey
- 4 cups roughly chopped ripe Roma tomatoes
- 1 cup chopped peeled cucumber, plus more for serving
- ¼ cup chopped red bell pepper
- 2 small cloves garlic
- ¼ cup sherry vinegar or red wine vinegar
- 3 tablespoons extra-virgin olive oil
- 1 teaspoon salt
- ½ teaspoon black pepper
- Croutons for serving

WHICH WHEY?
BEST Acid, sweet
GOOD Cooked

1 Tear the bread into small pieces and soak it in a small bowl with the whey while you prepare the rest of the ingredients.

2 Add the whey and bread mixture, tomatoes, cucumber, bell pepper, garlic, vinegar, oil, salt, and black pepper to a blender. Blend until you like the texture. Less than a minute is usually plenty for me. I like to detect just a little of the cucumber and bread texture.

3 Taste for seasoning, and add more salt, black pepper, and vinegar as desired. Transfer to a pitcher and chill in the refrigerator for 2 hours.

4 To serve, pour the gazpacho into bowls and top with croutons and more chopped cucumber.

Refrigerate leftover soup and enjoy within 5 days.

Elote
(Mexican Grilled Corn)

Elote just means "corn" in Spanish, but it has become the name for this dressed-up street snack famous in Mexico. If you have ever smelled corn on the grill, you will understand the nostalgia that comes with that scent, which may remind you of a late-summer meal at home or of a trip to Mexico.

Simmering the corn in whey first makes it extra sweet, buttery, and juicy, all wonderful qualities in grilled corn and especially nice for this preparation. The corn can be served speared on large bamboo skewers, or the kernels can be scraped off the cob and all the toppings piled on top. You can even cut the cobs in half for appetizer-size mini cobs that will leave everyone wanting more!

YIELD 6 servings ••• **TIME** 40 minutes

INGREDIENTS

- 2 quarts whey
- 6 ears corn, husked and trimmed
- 1 teaspoon sea salt
- 2 tablespoons butter
- ¼ cup mayonnaise or sour cream, or a combination
- ½ cup crumbled cotija cheese or grated Parmesan cheese
- 3 tablespoons finely chopped cilantro
- 2 teaspoons chili powder
- 2 limes, cut into wedges
  Hot sauce or adobo sauce for serving, optional

WHICH WHEY?
BEST Cooked, sweet
OKAY Acid

1 Put the whey, corn, and salt in a large pot over high heat. Bring to a boil, then cook the corn for just 1 minute more. Turn off the heat. Remove the corn from the pot and pat dry. Brush it with butter. (Use the whey for a soup, like Cream of Broccoli Soup [page 74], or freeze it for later use.)

2 Heat a grill or cast-iron skillet over medium-high heat. Grill the corn, checking and turning often, for about 5 minutes. Do not allow the corn to dry out too much. You want a few toasty bits and caramelization. Place the corn on a serving platter.

3 Brush the cobs with the mayonnaise and sprinkle with the cheese, cilantro, and chili powder. Serve immediately with lime wedges for squeezing and your favorite hot sauce for more heat. I like adding adobo sauce from canned chipotles in adobo.

Leta's Orecchiette Pasta
with Spring Vegetables

Leta Merrill is the master pasta maker at Pasta Maia, a business she founded here in Portland, Oregon. She also teaches classes, so we teamed up to teach a pasta and cheese class using ricotta and whey to make hand-shaped pasta. The resourcefulness of her approach was right up my alley, and I asked Leta then and there to contribute a recipe for this book (even though it was only a twinkle in my eye at the time).

Leta used cooked whey from cow's milk ricotta to develop this recipe, and I really enjoy using sweet whey. Leta does note that the acidity of yogurt whey could also be used to give the pasta a pleasant sourdough flavor you just won't find in store-bought pasta. And don't let the handmade aspect intimidate you. With practice your hands will understand the shaping motion, and the sweet shape (*orecchiette* means "little ear" in Italian) holds this spring vegetable sauce (or any sauce) beautifully. If you have a scale, weigh the flour, as Leta does, for best results.

YIELD 4 servings ••• **TIME** 1½ hours, 1 hour active

FOR THE PASTA

500	grams (1 pound 2 ounces) semolina rimacinata flour, plus more for sprinkling
250	grams whey (8 fluid ounces)

FOR THE SAUCE

4	tablespoons butter
2	medium shallots or 1 leek, sliced into thin rings
	Salt
1½	cups thinly sliced seasonal mushrooms
1	cup dry white wine or whey
1½	cups 1-inch pieces sugar snap peas or asparagus, cut on a bias
2	tablespoons thinly sliced mint leaves, plus more for garnish (optional)
½	cup ricotta cheese or full-fat yogurt
1	cup pea shoots or arugula for garnish

WHICH WHEY?
BEST Cooked, sweet
GOOD Acid

SPECIAL EQUIPMENT

- Food scale
- Bench scraper
- Spray bottle filled with water

Semolina rimacinata flour is a refined version of durum wheat flour. This flour is a traditional ingredient in hand-formed pasta of southern Italy and results in a pleasantly sweet, al dente pasta.

1   **MAKE THE PASTA.** Pile the flour in a mound on a board. Make a well in the center and add almost all of the whey. With a fork, slowly incorporate the liquid into the flour until a paste forms.

2   When most of the flour has been incorporated, use a bench scraper to bring the remaining flour and whey together. Use a "chopping" motion to distribute the whey. With your hands, begin to squeeze the dough together, adding the remaining whey in small amounts to dry areas.

3   Once the dough begins to come together, stop adding whey, and use your hands to coax the dough into a ball. Knead until it's smooth and elastic, 5 to 10 minutes. If the dough is too dry, spritz it with water. If the dough is too wet, sprinkle the work surface with flour and incorporate the flour into the dough while kneading.

4   The dough is sufficiently kneaded when it appears smooth and it springs back to the touch. Cover the dough and allow it to rest for 30 minutes on the countertop or up to overnight, refrigerated.

5   **MAKE THE SAUCE.** Melt the butter in a large skillet over medium heat and add the shallots. Season with salt and cook until the shallots are softened, about 4 minutes. Add the mushrooms to the pan, season with more salt, and cook, stirring occasionally, until the mushrooms have released all of their water and have begun to caramelize, about 8 minutes. Deglaze the pan with the wine and increase the heat to high. Reduce the liquid by half, then remove the pan from the heat. Set the vegetables aside until the pasta is done cooking.

continued on next page

6 SHAPE THE PASTA. After the dough has rested, cut off a small portion, and cover the remaining dough. With your hands, roll the portion of dough into a long snake about the diameter of your thumb.

7 Using a butter knife, cut the dough snake into cubes.

8 Position one cube of dough to look like a diamond, and lay the butter knife horizontally over the top corner of the diamond. Press down on the blade with your index finger to flatten the cube and drag it across the board, creating a hollowed disk.

9 Gently push the hollowed disk over the tip of your thumb to create a small dome. Repeat this process with the remaining dough.

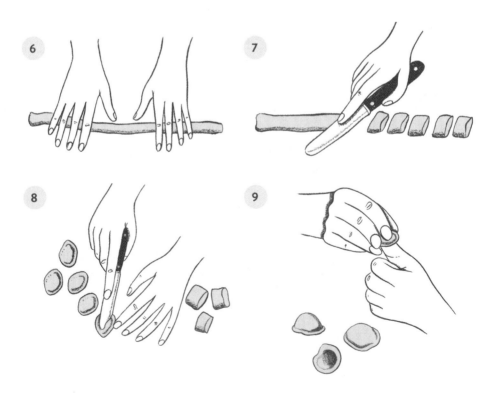

10 COOK THE PASTA. Bring a large pot of water to a rapid boil. Salt the water generously and cook the pasta until it floats and is al dente, 3 to 6 minutes. Reserving 1 cup of the pasta cooking water, drain the pasta and add it to the mushroom mixture. Add ½ cup pasta cooking water and stir in the sugar snap peas. Cook over medium-high heat until the sauce thickens and coats the pasta, adding more pasta water if necessary.

11 Remove the pan from the heat and stir in the mint and ricotta. Taste for seasoning and add more salt if needed. Serve the pasta in shallow bowls garnished with pea shoots and more mint if desired.

You can store uncooked shaped pasta for up to 3 days, uncovered in the refrigerator on a baking sheet lined with a towel and sprinkled with flour. Alternatively, freeze the pasta in a single layer on a baking sheet, then transfer it to a sealed container and store in the freezer for up to 6 months.

Cathy's Soubise-Style Risotto

Described as a channeler of the soul, psyche, and techniques of Italy, Chef Cathy Whims is a master of inventive regional Italian cuisine. Cathy introduced me to soubise, which is a cream sauce thickened with a good amount of sautéed onions. This risotto features three members of the onion family—leeks, green garlic (harvested early in the growing season), and spring onions. With the addition of fresh chervil, it really captures the goodness of spring. Cathy developed this recipe using acid whey from cow's milk yogurt.

With Cathy guiding me through my first attempt at making risotto, it came out beautifully and was not at all the fussy dish I anticipated. I look forward to trying different flavor combinations as the seasons change.

YIELD 4 servings ••• **TIME** 40 minutes

INGREDIENTS

- 5 leeks, trimmed and sliced
- 7 cups whey*
- 1 tablespoon butter
- 1 cup finely chopped spring bulb onion
- 3 tablespoons chopped green garlic
- ½ teaspoon salt
- 2 cups Arborio or Carnaroli rice
- ½ cup white wine
- 1½ teaspoons tomato paste
- Freshly ground black pepper
- ½ cup grated Parmigiano-Reggiano cheese
- ¼ cup chervil leaves or combinations of parsley and fennel fronds

*Or at least 1 cup whey plus enough water to equal 7 cups of liquid

WHICH WHEY?
BEST Acid
GOOD Sweet, cooked

1   Put the leeks and the whey in a large pot and bring to a strong simmer over high heat. Cook until the leeks are somewhat softened, about 10 minutes. Reduce the heat to low and remove the leeks from the broth with a slotted spoon (they can be eaten with the risotto, if desired). Leave the broth on low heat to keep warm.

2   While the broth simmers, melt the butter in a skillet over medium-high heat. When the foaming subsides, add the onion, garlic, and salt. Cook, stirring occasionally, until the onion is softened.

3   Add the rice and stir until the rice is completely coated in butter. Sauté until it turns translucent and gives off a roasted, starchy aroma. Do not let the onion brown.

4   Add the wine and bring to a gentle simmer (not a rolling boil). Lower the heat to medium and stir in 1 cup of the broth and the tomato paste.

5   Cook, stirring often but not constantly, making sure to move all the rice from the bottom and sides of the pan. When most of the liquid is absorbed, add another ladleful or two of broth and continue cooking until that amount is absorbed. The rice should always be loose, but not too wet or too dry.

    Repeat until the rice is plump and creamy. When the risotto is done, it should remain a bit wet, with some liquid still apparent around the edges of the pan.

6   Remove from the heat and season with pepper and additional salt to taste. Top with the cheese and chervil and serve immediately.

Our Holiday Potato Salad

I don't remember when my family started including potato salad on our holiday menus, but we all look forward to it as much as the main dishes. My sister Noemy is the recipe keeper; her potato salad alongside our Christmas tamales is a must. My nieces always request a large batch so that's what this is. You can cut the recipe in half if you don't have a mob of potato salad lovers coming over for a holiday feast.

This recipe is likely not that different from your family's version, but my sister says the trick with the egg yolks makes a big difference, and for me, it's not right without celery and black olives. Cooking the potatoes in sweet whey adds a layer of creaminess that is lovely in many potato dishes (I've also tried it with mashed and scalloped!).

YIELD 20 servings ··· **TIME** 1 hour

INGREDIENTS

- 10 large russet potatoes, peeled and cut in half
- 3 quarts sweet whey, or more if needed
- 1 bunch celery, trimmed and diced
- 1 bunch scallions, trimmed and sliced
- 1 (6-ounce) can sliced black olives, drained
- 6 hard-boiled eggs, peeled
- 1–2 cups mayonnaise
- 1 tablespoon yellow mustard

  Salt and black pepper

WHICH WHEY?
BEST Sweet, cooked
OKAY Acid

1. Add the potatoes to a large pot and cover with the whey, adding more whey or water if needed. Bring to a boil and cook until the potatoes are so tender they fall apart when poked with a fork. Drain the potatoes in a colander and let them cool.

2. Add the celery, scallions, and olives to a large bowl. Remove the yolks from the eggs and set them aside. Dice the egg whites and add them to the bowl with the vegetables. Cube the potatoes and stir them into the vegetables.

3. Add 1 cup mayonnaise and the mustard and mix them in. It's okay if the potatoes mash a bit along the way. That's what we want. Add salt and pepper to taste. Adjust the mayonnaise to your preference, and at the very end, crumble the egg yolks on top of the potato salad. The salad can be eaten immediately but is best chilled for at least 1 hour.

If you have leftovers, refrigerate and eat within 3 days.

When you drain the potatoes, catch the starchy whey in a large bowl. It can be used for soups like Cream of Broccoli Soup (page 74). Cool and store in the refrigerator for up to 5 days or freeze for up to 6 months.

Tahini-Garlic Dressing

Have you ever had that thick, tangy, garlicky sauce often served in Lebanese restaurants? That's what this dressing reminds me of. It satisfies that craving for a cream dressing without mayonnaise and is so worth whipping up regularly to have on hand. It will make it easy to eat more veggies but also works beautifully on meats and grains. I like making this dressing with acid whey because of the extra tang and because it lasts longer without spoiling. Feel free to change this up with a handful of your favorite fresh herbs.

YIELD 1 cup

INGREDIENTS

- 1 cup whey
- ½ cup tahini
- ¼ cup lemon juice
- 2 tablespoons olive oil
- 2 cloves garlic
- 1 teaspoon ground sumac or grated lemon zest
- ½ teaspoon sea salt
- ½ teaspoon dried oregano
- ¼ cup packed fresh herbs, such as parsley, cilantro, and/or dill, optional

WHICH WHEY?
BEST Acid
GOOD Sweet, cooked

1 Put ½ cup of the whey in a blender with the tahini, lemon juice, oil, garlic, sumac, salt, and oregano. Start the blender at low speed and move up to medium speed, blending until the dressing is smooth and emulsified. If the blender needs more liquid to work, or if the sauce is looking more like a thick dip than a salad dressing, add some of the remaining whey a little at a time until you like the consistency after blending. It will get a little thicker when it's chilled.

2 Add the herbs, if desired, and pulse for a few seconds or until you like the size of the bits.

Transfer the dressing to a jar or bottle and store in the refrigerator. Enjoy within 3 weeks if you used acid whey or 1 week with other types.

Lighter Alfredo Sauce

This magical sauce tastes like cream and cheese even though it contains neither. I learned to combine nuts, starches, and spices strategically when developing my dairy-free line of cheese kits and sauce mixes as well as writing my book *One-Hour Dairy-Free Cheese*. Those recipes don't contain whey, of course, but adding it here makes the dairy effect even more convincing. You can sprinkle in some (or a lot) of your favorite cheese at the very end, but the sauce is luscious as is.

YIELD 2 cups ••• **TIME** 15 minutes

INGREDIENTS

- 1½ cups whey
- ½ cup blanched almond flour or 1 cup soaked raw cashews*
- 3 tablespoons olive oil (any kind you enjoy)
- 3 tablespoons tapioca starch
- 2 tablespoons lemon juice or red wine vinegar (can omit if you use acid whey)
- 1 tablespoon nutritional yeast, optional
- 1 clove garlic
- 1 teaspoon sea salt
- ½ teaspoon onion powder
- ½ teaspoon dried Italian herb blend
- ½ teaspoon mustard powder or 1 teaspoon Dijon mustard
- ¼ teaspoon white pepper

WHICH WHEY?
BEST Cooked, acid
GOOD Sweet

1. Add all the ingredients to a blender and process at high speed until the mixture is silky and smooth. Be especially observant of the nuts—you don't want this sauce to be grainy.

2. Transfer the mixture to a pot and cook over medium heat. As the sauce begins to simmer, it will start to thicken dramatically, starting at the bottom of the pot. Use a scraper to constantly stir the thicker sauce up from the bottom, blending it into the rest of the sauce until it's all thickened. This should take about 7 minutes. Adjust the seasoning to taste.

3. Feel free to thin the sauce with more whey as needed, but keep in mind that the sauce will get a little thinner when you add it to wet pasta.

Use the sauce immediately or store in a jar in the refrigerator and use within 1 week. Reheat the sauce in a small saucepan and whisk in water or whey as needed to make the sauce silky smooth again and thin to your desired consistency.

*If using cashews, cover them with water and soak for at least 4 hours and up to 12 hours, or simmer them for 20 minutes to soften. Drain.

Bean and Queso Dip

This cheesy sauce and bean dip combination is a nourishing answer to those nacho cravings. It's hard to believe you can make a hearty queso dip without actual cheese, but the white beans combine with the whey and tapioca starch to give it the right texture, and the nutritional yeast adds a sharp cheesy flavor. Don't stop at nachos though—this sauce is great on pasta, hamburgers, baked potatoes, and roasted vegetables.

YIELD 2 cups ••• **TIME** 15 minutes

INGREDIENTS

- 1½ cups whey
- 1 (15-ounce) can or 1½ cups home-cooked white beans, such as cannellini or navy beans
- ½ cup salsa or fire-roasted tomatoes and chiles, diced
- 3 tablespoons tapioca starch
- 2 tablespoons avocado oil or other neutral oil
- 2 tablespoons nutritional yeast
- 2 tablespoons lime juice or apple cider vinegar (can omit if you use acid whey)
- ¼ cup chopped onion
- 1 teaspoon sea salt
- ½ teaspoon garlic powder
- ½ teaspoon chili powder
- ½ teaspoon smoked paprika

WHICH WHEY?
BEST Sweet, cooked
GOOD Acid

1 Combine all the ingredients in a blender and blend on high speed until creamy and smooth.

2 Transfer the mixture to a pot and cook over medium heat. As the sauce begins to simmer, it will start to thicken dramatically, starting at the bottom of the pot. Use a scraper to constantly stir the thicker sauce up from the bottom, blending it into the rest of the sauce until it's all thickened. This should take about 7 minutes. Adjust the seasoning to taste.

Use the sauce immediately or pour into a jar and store in the refrigerator for up 1 week. To reheat the sauce, pour it into a small saucepan and whisk in water or whey as needed to make the sauce silky smooth again and thin to your desired consistency. I don't recommend freezing it.

Brunost
(Norwegian Brown Cheese)

This recipe isn't easy to classify, but I had to include it because Norwegian brunost, or "brown cheese," is the food I am asked about most often when I say I make things out of whey. Not a cheese in the technical sense, it starts off as if you are making whey ricotta (see page 22) but is cooked down for much longer. Called gjetost if made from goat's milk whey and mysost if made from cow's milk whey, this cheeselike food is basically caramelized whey with a fudgelike texture, toasty color, and savory, umami flavor.

Traditionally brunost is eaten for breakfast with jam, but you can enjoy it any time. Some people describe it as an acquired taste, but I loved it from the start and eat it before or after dinner, just like cheese. Serve it on seeded bread or rustic crackers, with jam or with fruit.

Your results will vary in flavor and texture depending on the whey you use, so experimenting with this recipe can be a lot of fun. This makes a small batch because it takes a long time to cook the liquid out of whey (you can even cut it in half if you don't have four hours). You can certainly simmer a larger amount of whey if you happen to have someplace, such as the top of a wood-burning stove, where you can leave it to cook all day.

YIELD About ¾ cup ••• **TIME** 4 hours

INGREDIENTS

- 1 quart whey
- ¼ cup heavy cream

WHICH WHEY?
BEST Sweet
OKAY Acid, cooked

The goal is a thick fudgelike "cheese" you can slice thinly. This may take practice! It's tempting to cook the whey longer, but it's best to stop a little early and wind up with a spreadable product rather than the dry crumbles that result if you overcook it. But either way, it's a delicious, unique treat.

1   Butter a 1-cup ramekin or small bowl and set it aside.

2   Simmer the whey in a heavy pot over medium-low heat until it thickens to the texture of oatmeal or loose ricotta. Stir occasionally to make sure the solids aren't sticking to the pot. The whey will take at least 3 hours to thicken sufficiently. At this point it will be beige, not brown.

3   Add the cream to the thickened whey and continue to simmer for 15 to 20 minutes, stirring continously to prevent sticking and burning. The mixture will caramelize, thicken, and brown more.

4   When the brunost is thick but spreadable and has the shiny texture of caramel, scoop it into the prepared ramekin and allow it to cool. It will thicken more as it cools. Use as a spread or, if it is firm enough, turn it out of the ramekin and cut it into thin slices.

Store well wrapped in the refrigerator. Enjoy within 1 month.

Nicole's Duck Ramen

This recipe is another contribution by Nicole Easterday, who also shared her Nicole's Lemon Meringue Pie Cocktail (page 48). Here she uses sweet whey from a cow's milk cheese in ramen stock to add a richness and slight sweetness that you don't get with plain water. The mouthfeel is like gelatin-rich bone broth. I highly recommend it. I tried it with guinea fowl instead of duck and it was incredible.

YIELD 4 servings ••• **TIME** 4 hours, 45 minutes active

FOR THE BONE BROTH

	Bones and skin from 1 whole roasted duck or chicken (meat removed and reserved for serving)
3	Chinese onions or leeks, split lengthwise
4	large carrots, split lengthwise
	4-inch piece fresh ginger, split lengthwise
1	head garlic, cloves separated
	Vegetable oil for brushing and roasting
4–5	shiitake mushrooms, fresh or dried
2	star anise pods
4–6	cups whey
8–10	cups water

FOR THE RAMEN

3	quarts bone broth
3	tablespoons soy sauce
2	tablespoons dashi powder
2	tablespoons mirin
2	tablespoons fish sauce
30	ounces uncooked ramen noodles
3	tablespoons miso paste

WHICH WHEY?
BEST Sweet
GOOD Acid, cooked

1 **MAKE THE BROTH.** Spread the bones and skin, onions, carrots, ginger, and garlic on a baking sheet, brush lightly with oil, and place under the broiler until browned.

2 Combine the roasted bones, skin, and vegetables with the mushrooms, star anise, and whey in a large stockpot. Add enough water to cover the ingredients. Cover the pot and bring to a boil.

3 Reduce the heat and simmer for 2 to 3 hours, adding more water as needed. Strain through a fine-mesh sieve. Return to the pot, bring back to a boil, and reduce until you have about 3 quarts liquid.

4 **MAKE THE RAMEN.** Add the soy sauce, dashi powder, mirin, and fish sauce to the broth. Bring to a boil and add the noodles. Cook until the noodles are almost fully cooked (slightly firmer than al dente). Stir in the miso and add more soy sauce to taste.

5 Serve immediately, topped with medium-boiled eggs (a 7-minute boil to keep the yolks jammy), roasted duck meat, seaweed (like nori or dulse), corn (fresh or frozen), scallions, furikake, or whatever else you like in your ramen.

Lip-Smackin' Grilled Chicken Breast

Amchur is a powdered spice made from dried green mangoes, which is used in Indian cooking and, along with whey, makes this chicken breast juicy and tender. I thank cookbook author and food reporter Priya Krishna for introducing me to amchur. Having been raised to add lime juice to just about everything imaginable, my eyes lit up the first time I tried its lip-smacking tang. If you don't have an Indian market near you, it's worth ordering the spice online. This dish is perfect with basmati rice and a fresh cucumber salad.

YIELD 4 servings ••• **TIME** 1½ hours, 30 minutes active

INGREDIENTS

- 2 cups whey
- 2 tablespoons lemon juice, plus more for serving
- 4 cloves garlic, minced
- 2 tablespoons minced fresh ginger
- 2 tablespoons olive oil, plus more for serving
- 1 tablespoon ground turmeric
- 1 tablespoon ground coriander
- 1 tablespoon amchur
- 1 teaspoon red chili powder or paprika
- 1 teaspoon sea salt
- 4 boneless, skinless chicken breasts
- ¼ cup finely chopped cilantro for serving

WHICH WHEY?
BEST Acid
GOOD Sweet
OKAY Cooked

1 Whisk together the whey, lemon juice, garlic, ginger, oil, turmeric, coriander, amchur, chili powder, and salt in a pan and add the chicken breasts to mostly, or fully, submerge them in the brine. Allow the chicken to sit in brine for 1 hour in the refrigerator. Flip halfway through to make sure all sides are evenly brined.

2 Heat a grill to high and brush the grates with oil. Grill the chicken until it reaches an internal temperature of 155°F (68°C), about 3 minutes on each side. You want it to remain juicy.

3 Once cooked, let the chicken rest for 10 minutes before slicing.

4 To serve, top with cilantro, a sprinkling of chili powder, and drizzles of oil and lemon juice.

If you don't brine the chicken for a full hour, this dish will still be delicious. The lemon juice, ginger, and, if you use it, yogurt whey add layers of flavor. The whey brine makes the chicken really juicy. You can use any cuts that you like.

Ghee-Fried Chicken .

If you are accustomed to frying in canola oil, you may think that using ghee (clarified butter) isn't a necessary substitution, but I promise you, one crunchy, buttery bite will change your mind. Ghee is available in specialty grocery stores, or you can make it yourself in a snap.

Brining chicken for frying is a long-held tradition for good reason. The chicken ends up moist and juicy, which is such a great contrast to the crispy fried batter. Whey of any kind will behave a lot like buttermilk when brining chicken.

As for the batter, I had a lot of fun testing the Colonel's "11 secret herbs and spices" published by the *Chicago Tribune*, but in the end, I went for delicious simplicity. You can play with the spices for variety or to create your own secret recipe. Try swapping in sweet paprika or garlic powder instead of onion powder, or add thyme or perhaps some celery salt.

YIELD 4–6 servings ••• **TIME** 3 hours, 45 minutes active

INGREDIENTS

- 2 tablespoons smoked paprika
- 2 teaspoons onion powder
- 2 teaspoons dried oregano
- 1 teaspoon white pepper or 2 teaspoons black pepper
- ½ teaspoon cayenne pepper
- 2½ teaspoons sea salt
- 2 cups whey
- 1 large egg
- 1½ cups all-purpose flour
- ¼ cup ghee, or more as needed
- 6 chicken thighs and/or drumsticks or 1 whole chicken cut into pieces
- Lemon wedges for serving, optional
- Honey for serving, optional

WHICH WHEY?
BEST Any type

1 Mix the paprika, onion powder, oregano, pepper, and cayenne with ½ teaspoon of the salt in a small bowl. Whisk the whey and egg with half of the spice mixture in a shallow dish. In a pie plate or other shallow dish, add the flour and remaining 2 teaspoons salt to the remaining spice mix and stir to combine. Cover and set aside.

2 Add the chicken pieces to the whey mixture, turning to coat on all sides. Refrigerate the chicken for at least 1 hour or up to overnight. Flip the chicken halfway through so it brines evenly. Remove the chicken from the refrigerator and let it rest at room temperature for 30 minutes before frying it.

3 When you are ready to cook, set a wire rack over a baking sheet near the stove. Heat the ghee in a heavy pan over medium-high heat until a drop of water sizzles on it. When you get that sizzle, reduce the heat to medium. Remove one piece of chicken from the brine,

allowing the excess brine to drip off. Dredge the chicken in the flour mixture, turning and patting to coat generously for a nice crunchy crust. Repeat with two more pieces, and place the pieces carefully in the hot ghee. (Frying in batches ensures that the oil stays hot and all the chicken cooks evenly.)

4 Fry until the chicken is medium golden brown, turning each piece once. Each batch will take about 15 minutes to cook, depending on the size and what part you are using. Chicken on the bone takes the longest. Cook until a meat thermometer reads 165°F (74°C) in the thickest part of the thigh (alternatively, poke the pieces and look for clear liquid).

5 Transfer the fried pieces to the wire rack. Add more ghee to the pan as needed, and make sure it's hot before frying more chicken. Repeat with the remaining chicken pieces. I often serve this fried chicken with lemon wedges, but a drizzle of warm honey is also incredible with the ghee.

HOW TO MAKE GHEE

1 Melt 1 stick butter in a small saucepan and bring to a boil over medium heat. Watch carefully, because you don't want the butter to brown.

2 Immediately reduce the heat to low and simmer gently for 5 minutes to allow some moisture to evaporate and to separate the white solids from the golden fat—this is important for storage and use.

3 Remove the pan from the heat and let it sit for 15 minutes so that all the solids to drop to the bottom of the pan. Strain through a double layer of fine-mesh cheesecloth. The golden clarified butter is ghee. The few solids that remain are salty and delicious on rice.

You can store the ghee at room temperature indefinitely and use it to cook with high heat.

Baja Shrimp Cocktail

Oh, how I miss the soupy, spicy seafood cocktails of my childhood. Growing up close to Baja California, Mexico, I enjoyed all sorts of delicious seafood. This recipe uses whey to combine the flavors and textures of my favorite lime-rich shrimp cocktails and ceviche.

You might even think of it as a seafood salsa, pico de gallo–style. You can scoop up juicy bites using tortilla chips, though tostadas and simple salted crackers work, too. The whey tenderizes the shrimp, giving it a great ceviche-like texture while enhancing the other flavors, especially if you use acid whey. Try to find a Mexican hot sauce such as Tapatio for serving.

YIELD 8 servings ••• **TIME** 1½ hours, 30 minutes active

INGREDIENTS

- 2 pounds peeled and deveined raw shrimp, any kind
- 1 clove garlic, minced
- ½ teaspoon sea salt
- 1 cup whey
- ½ cup lime juice
- ½ cup diced white onion
- 2 tablespoons ketchup or ¼ cup canned tomato sauce
- 1 serrano or jalapeño chile, diced
- 1 cup diced cucumber
- 1 cup diced Roma tomato
- 1 cup diced avocado
- ½ cup packed chopped cilantro
- Tapatio hot sauce, optional
- Lime wedges for serving

WHICH WHEY?
BEST Acid
GOOD Sweet, cooked

1 Cook the shrimp with the garlic and salt in a skillet over medium heat, tossing until the shrimp just turn pink and the garlic gets a little soft, 4 minutes. The shrimp will release some liquid. Transfer the shrimp to a bowl and allow to cool for 15 minutes.

2 While the shrimp cool, combine the whey, lime juice, onion, ketchup, and chile in a small bowl. Pour the brine over the cooled shrimp and toss to combine. Place in the refrigerator for at least 30 minutes or up to 1 hour.

3 Right before serving, add the cucumber, tomato, avocado, and cilantro. Serve with hot sauce if you like and, of course, extra wedges of lime.

It's best to enjoy this the same day, as the veggies can get soft, but you can push it to 2 days. Store in the refrigerator.

Broth-Poached Salmon

A French-style court bouillon is an aromatic broth used to quickly poach fish and chicken. Using whey instead of water for the broth makes the fish even more tender and flaky, and it's hard to mess up. All of the benefits of the original method—plus the richness of whey with its lactic acid—make this a recipe you will return to again and again.

If you have ever been frustrated by dry, overcooked fish, you will especially like this method of cooking. As a bonus, you get a flavorful broth to enjoy as a simple soup along with your fish or in a seafood chowder.

YIELD 4 servings ••• **TIME** 20 minutes

INGREDIENTS

- 4 cups whey
- ½ cup dry white wine
- 1 carrot, sliced
- 1 onion, sliced
- 2 ribs celery, sliced
- ½ teaspoon cracked peppercorns
- 1 bay leaf
- Peel of ½ lemon (reserve juice for serving)
- A handful fresh herbs, such as parsley, cilantro, thyme, dill, or celery leaves
- 4 skin-on salmon fillets
- Sea salt
- 2 tablespoons melted butter or ghee
- 2 tablespoons lemon juice or lemon slices

WHICH WHEY?
BEST Any type

1. Add the whey, wine, carrot, onion, celery, peppercorns, bay leaf, lemon peel, and herbs to a baking dish and bring to a boil. Reduce the heat to medium low and simmer for 10 minutes to cook the veggies lightly and infuse the whey.

2. Turn the heat to the lowest setting. When all bubbling subsides, add as many of the salmon fillets as will fit without overlapping. The broth should cover the fish. Cook in two batches if necessary.

3. Cover the dish and cook the fish for 5 minutes. Check the fish; it should be flaky and opaque pink, no longer glossy pink. If it's not done, cook for another 2 or 3 minutes—check the smallest pieces first. Although the fish cooks quickly, poaching is a forgiving method that doesn't overcook fish as easily as baking does.

4. Remove each fillet as soon as it is cooked and place on a serving platter. Sprinkle with salt, melted butter, and lemon juice before serving. If you plan to enjoy them as a side dish, season the broth and vegetables with salt and lemon juice.

Sweets

As with beverages, whey adds a silky creaminess and body to sweets. It can take the place of milk or water and even serve as a sweetener (see Sweetened Condensed Whey, page 104). Used strategically, whey can lighten recipes or add richness. Furthermore, it adds complex flavors that can be a lot of fun to play with when making things like caramel, pies, curd, and ice pops.

Sarah's Lemon Curd

In addition to being a professional hot sauce maker, Sarah Marshall of Marshall's Haute Sauce is a social worker with a passion for social justice. She teaches canning workshops and writes cookbooks, including *Preservation Pantry: Modern Canning from Root to Top & Stem to Core* in which she uses fruits and vegetables in creative ways.

Given her resourcefulness, I knew Sarah would have a great use for whey! I adore lemon curd, and her version—which incorporates cooked whey from ricotta along with honey and coconut oil—is especially exciting.

YIELD 4 cups ••• **TIME** 2 hours 45 minutes, 35 minutes active

INGREDIENTS

3–4	large lemons
8	egg yolks
1½	cups whey
½	cup butter
½	cup coconut oil
½	cup honey

WHICH WHEY?
BEST Cooked
GOOD Sweet, acid

SPECIAL EQUIPMENT

• Four 8-ounce storage jars with lids

Use the leftover egg whites for an omelette or a meringue or as a coating when making spiced nuts. Egg whites freeze nicely for up to 6 months.

1 Rinse the lemons under cold running water and towel dry. Zest all the lemons with a Microplane, avoiding the white pith. Cut the lemons in half and juice enough to produce ½ cup juice.

2 Bring 3 cups water to a boil in a medium pot. Adjust the heat to keep it at a low simmer.

3 Whisk the lemon juice, all the zest, the egg yolks, and the whey in a large, heatproof glass bowl until thoroughly combined.

4 Place the bowl on top of the pot of hot water and stir constantly with a spatula for 5 minutes. It's important to keep the mixture moving to avoid curdling the egg yolks.

5 Add the butter and cook, stirring, for 5 minutes longer. Add the oil and cook, stirring, for 5 minutes longer.

6 Slowly drizzle in the honey, and whisk until the curd is thick, 5 to 10 minutes. Remove from the heat and run through a fine-mesh strainer.

7 Scoop the curd into the jars and allow to cool at room temperature for about 20 minutes. Cover and refrigerate for 2 hours minimum to set.

Store in the refrigerator for up to 10 days.

Pineapple Soft Serve

This quick soft serve is great for when you want a frozen treat without having to wait hours for homemade ice pops or ice cream to freeze. It's a simple dessert, but the whey and tropical pineapple create a lovely flavor combination. Add a splash of coconut milk and it may remind you of a pineapple whip tasted on a tropical vacation. This base recipe is flexible, so if you don't have frozen pineapple on hand, swap in any frozen fruit.

YIELD 4 servings

INGREDIENTS

- 4 cups frozen pineapple chunks
- 1 cup whey
- ¼ cup coconut milk or coconut cream, optional
- 2 tablespoons honey or other sweetener, optional*

*Added sweetener should only be necessary when using supertart acid whey or when the fruit is not very ripe.

WHICH WHEY?
BEST Sweet
GOOD Cooked, acid

1 Add the pineapple, whey, and coconut milk, if using, to a food processor and process on high speed until the mixture is completely smooth. You may have to stop and scrape the sides of the bowl a couple of times. A blender will also do the job, but the result is more like a smoothie than soft serve.

2 Taste and add sweetener if needed. Process again. Serve immediately.

Store leftover soft serve in the freezer, where it will freeze solid. Let it defrost for 15 minutes at room temperature before serving. The texture won't be quite the same, but it will still be good.

Mango-Coconut Sherbert

My editor tells me that "sherbet" and "sherbert" are both correct, so I'm sticking with the way I've said it all my life! Spelling aside, I have loved sherbert since I tasted "rainbow flavor" in those fun pops you push up as you lick. In this version, the whey blends beautifully with the tangy mango, and the rich coconut cream gives the frozen mixture a nice texture. The orange makes it taste more like sherbert to me, but it's optional. If you have reusable ice-pop molds, use them to make this delicious dessert even more fun to eat.

YIELD 1 quart ••• **TIME** 4 hours, 15 minutes active

INGREDIENTS

- 3 cups whey
- 1½ cups mango chunks, fresh or frozen and thawed
- 1 cup coconut cream (see note)
- ½ cup honey
- 2 tablespoons orange juice, optional
- 1 teaspoon orange zest, optional

WHICH WHEY?
BEST Sweet, acid
OKAY Cooked

SPECIAL EQUIPMENT

- Shallow quart-size container with a lid or ice-pop molds

1 Add the whey, mango, coconut cream, honey, orange juice, and orange zest, if using, to a blender and process until smooth. Mangos vary in flavor depending on their degree of ripeness, so taste the mixture for sweetness and tartness levels and adjust to your taste by adding a little more honey and/or orange juice if needed.

2 Pour the mixture into a container or into ice-pop molds. Freeze for 3 to 4 hours or until solid. Allow to sit at room temperature for 10 to 15 minutes before scooping. (Ice pops can be eaten straight out of the freezer, but dip the molds into a cup of warm water to release them.)

Enjoy within 2 months.

If you can't find coconut cream, only coconut milk, place 2 cans in the refrigerator the night before, so the cream separates completely. To measure the cream, open 1 can and drain off the watery portion. (Use it to make a smoothie or cook rice or oatmeal. Think of it as coconut whey!) Scrape the thick coconut cream that remains into a measuring cup. Brands vary in cream content, so if necessary, open another can to make a full cup.

Berries and Cream Ice Pops

A little bit cheesecake, a little bit pie, these berry ice pops are a lot yummy. The whey lightens up what could be a really rich frozen treat while still adding plenty of milky goodness. The addition of cookie chunks makes these pops extra special. Use whatever berries are in season or go with frozen, which are picked at the height of flavor.

The whey you use makes a difference here. An acid whey from yogurt adds tanginess, which may make you want to adjust the sweetener. You can skip the cream cheese, but it definitely elevates the taste, texture, and satisfaction factor.

YIELD 6 servings ••• **TIME** 5 hours, 15 minutes active

INGREDIENTS

- 3 cups berries, fresh or frozen and thawed
- 2 cups whey
- 4 ounces cream cheese (½ cup), optional
- ¼ cup sugar, honey, or your preferred sweetener
- 2 teaspoons vanilla extract
- 3 shortbread cookies or graham cracker halves, broken into pieces

WHICH WHEY?
BEST Sweet, acid
OKAY Cooked

SPECIAL EQUIPMENT
- 6 ice-pop molds

1 Add the berries, whey, cream cheese (if desired), sugar, and vanilla to a blender and process at medium speed until you see just a few small chunks of berries left. It's nice to leave some for texture.

2 Taste the mixture for sweetness and adjust depending on your preference and the ripeness of the berries. Blend again.

3 Pour the blended mix into the ice-pop molds, leaving a little room at the top. Add at least two bites of cookie to each mold. It's okay if the pieces float or even stick out a little. Add the ice-pop sticks and lids.

4 Transfer the molds to the freezer and allow the pops to freeze for at least 4 hours or until solid. This will depend on the size of the molds.

5 Before serving, dip each mold into a cup of warm water to help release it easily.

Wrap any remaining pops well, store in the freezer, and eat within 2 months.

Sweetened Condensed Whey (SCW)

SCW, as I came to call this recipe while developing it, is a nice trick to have in your back pocket for those times when you just don't know what to do with a lot of extra whey—simply add sugar and reduce it!

SCW is not so much a sweet to enjoy on its own but rather a replacement for sweetened condensed milk, sugar, syrups, or even honey in many recipes. The viscous consistency is useful in many instances, my favorite being how it helps frozen treats retain a nice texture right out of the freezer. Enjoy it in No-Churn Ice Cream (opposite), and use it to sweeten any frozen treats in this section. You will surely find your own nifty uses for it.

You can easily scale this recipe up for larger amounts of whey. You will extend the life of your whey dramatically without having to freeze it immediately. You will also reduce its volume so it will take up less space, and you'll have it whenever the need for a treat strikes.

YIELD 2 cups ••• **TIME** About an hour

INGREDIENTS

- 4 cups whey
- 1⅓ cups sugar

WHICH WHEY?
BEST Sweet, cooked
OKAY Acid

1 Place the whey in a heavy 1-quart pot and bring to a simmer over medium heat. Simmer until it reduces by a quarter, to about 1½ cups, about 10 minutes.

2 Strain the whey through a double layer of fine-mesh cheesecloth into a bowl, then return it to the pot. Add the sugar. Bring to a simmer over medium-low heat, stirring until the sugar is dissolved.

3 Stop stirring and continue to simmer over medium-low heat, avoiding a bubbling or rolling boil, until the whey reduces to 1 cup and coats the spoon like a thick syrup, 35 to 40 minutes. It will thicken more after chilling in the refrigerator.

4 Pour the SCW into a jar and allow to cool completely before putting on the lid.

Store, sealed, in the refrigerator and use within 4 months.

No-Churn Ice Cream

You won't believe the rich, smooth texture you can get without an ice cream maker. Two simple ingredients, whipping cream and Sweetened Condensed Whey (opposite), provide a base for endless variations. Vanilla is an obvious flavor to start with, but you can create custom flavors of this ice cream to suit your mood, the season, and special requests.

Try blueberry-almond, peanut-cajeta, raspberry–chocolate chip; any flavor is at your fingertips! I recommend making a large batch of SCW and keeping it in the fridge just for this purpose.

YIELD 1½ quarts ••• **TIME** 20 minutes, plus 5 hours freezing

INGREDIENTS

- 2 cups whipping cream or heavy cream, cold
- 1¾ cups Sweetened Condensed Whey (opposite)
- 2 teaspoons vanilla extract
- ¼–½ cup add-ins like Cajeta (page 107), chocolate chips, chopped nuts, crumbled cookies, or chopped fruit, optional

SPECIAL EQUIPMENT

- Freezer-safe container(s) with lid(s)

1 Beat the whipping cream with a hand mixer at medium speed until stiff peaks form.

2 Drizzle the sweetened condensed whey and the vanilla into the whipped cream. Beat at high speed until stiff peaks form again. This is your vanilla ice cream base. Mix in any desired flavorings now, either by hand or with a mixer. You can split the batch into separate containers to create different flavors.

3 Freeze in covered containers for at least 5 hours or overnight.

Enjoy within 3 weeks.

Hot Fudge Sauce

Hot fudge sauce, the kind that thickens like caramel when poured over ice cream, is one of my favorite foods on earth, especially when sprinkled with chopped peanuts. Making it at home is a revelation. The two types of chocolate and the butter do a great job of making it thick and deeply flavored. Using whey instead of cream lightens up this rich treat a bit.

This sauce is honestly wonderful eaten straight out of the jar with a spoon, but it is truly special with No-Churn Ice Cream (page 105) and Vanilla Poached Pears (page 111).

YIELD 2 cups ••• **TIME** 40 minutes

INGREDIENTS

- 2 cups whey
- 1½ cups sugar
- ¼ teaspoon sea salt
- ½ cup dark unsweetened cocoa powder
- 4 ounces unsweetened chocolate, finely chopped
- 5 tablespoons salted butter, cut into 10 pats
- 1 teaspoon vanilla extract

WHICH WHEY?
BEST Sweet
GOOD Cooked
OKAY Acid

1 Add the whey to a heavy 1-quart saucepan and simmer over medium heat until it is reduced by half. Stay close and check the bottom of the pan occasionally to avoid scorching. Lower the heat if necessary.

2 Line a colander with a double layer of fine-mesh cheesecloth and place over a medium bowl. Strain the whey to remove any solids.

3 Whisk the sugar and salt into the condensed whey to dissolve. Return the mixture to the pan and bring to a boil. Reduce the heat to a simmer and whisk in the cocoa powder until the mixture is smooth and fully blended. Continue to cook gently for 2 minutes.

4 Take the pan off the heat and stir in the chopped chocolate until partially melted. Let the mixture sit for 2 minutes longer to fully melt the chocolate. Whisk it to make sure no solid pieces remain.

5 Add pats of butter one at a time and whisk to melt each one before adding more. Finally, whisk in the vanilla extract.

Store in a jar in the refrigerator for up to 4 weeks. To rewarm, heat the sauce in the microwave in 15-second intervals, stirring in between, or heat in a small pan over low heat.

Cajeta (Mexican Caramel Sauce)

I grew up eating cajeta in Mexican candies. It is a spoonable caramel similar to dulce de leche. You can enjoy cajeta drizzled on ice cream (try it with No-Churn Ice Cream, page 105), spooned over apple pie or cheesecake, stirred into strong coffee, or served as a dip alongside sliced apples and a nice sharp cheese. Yum! If you have it, use goat's milk sweet whey. It is traditional and gives the cajeta a unique, complex flavor, but this recipe is equally wonderful made with cow's milk whey of any kind.

This is a supersimple beginner's caramel sauce. The baking soda is there to allow the whey to brown and caramelize without getting hard or burning, so there's no need for a candy thermometer. This method leaves you with a pourable but extra-dark and luscious sauce. If you haven't made caramel before and feel a little scared, you're about to impress yourself!

YIELD 1 cup ••• **TIME** 2 hours

INGREDIENTS

- 4 cups whey
- ½ vanilla bean or 1 teaspoon vanilla extract
- ¾ cup sugar
- 2 teaspoons baking soda
- Pinch sea salt

WHICH WHEY?
BEST Sweet
GOOD Cooked, acid

1 Pour the whey into a heavy 3-quart pot and bring to a boil. Line a colander with a double layer of fine-mesh cheesecloth and place it over a heavy 4-quart pot. Strain the whey to remove any solids.

2 Combine the vanilla bean with the clarified whey, sugar, baking soda, and salt in the pot. Cook over medium-low heat for 15 minutes, stirring to dissolve the sugar. The whey will get foamy and lighter in color. Scrape the sides of the pot frequently.

3 Continue cooking, stirring constantly to prevent scorching, until the whey is golden and has reduced by about three-quarters to a thick, sticky layer, about 45 minutes. You'll know it's ready when dragging the spoon across the bottom of the pot leaves a trail in the cajeta that lasts for 1 second.

4 Remove the pot from the heat. Scoop out the vanilla bean (great in a cup of hot chocolate!). Pour the cajeta into a heatproof jar and allow to cool for 30 minutes.

Store in a jar in the refrigerator for up to 2 months.

Linda's Honey Caramels

Linda Bangs co-owns Terra Farma, a livestock farm in Corbett, Oregon. She is a master in the kitchen and makes delicious truffles and caramels from the farm's milk. These taffylike, chewy caramels have a tangy flavor from the yogurt whey and a floral sweetness from the honey.

Linda developed this recipe using the acid whey from yogurt made from raw cow's milk, but just about any whey will work.

YIELD 64 caramels ••• **TIME** 3 hours, 30 minutes active

INGREDIENTS

- 6 cups whey
- 1½ cups sugar
- ⅓ cup honey
- 3 tablespoons butter
- 1 teaspoon vanilla extract
- Flake salt, optional

WHICH WHEY?
BEST Acid
GOOD Sweet
OKAY Cooked

SPECIAL EQUIPMENT

- Candy or digital thermometer
- Waxed paper

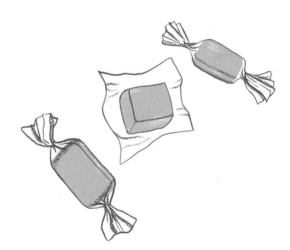

1   Pour the whey into a heavy 2-quart pot and bring to a simmer over medium heat. Continue to simmer until it reduces by a quarter (about 1½ cups of whey), 15 to 20 minutes.

2   Line a colander with a double layer of fine-mesh cheesecloth and place it over a heavy 4-quart pot. Use a large pot with tall sides, as the caramel will foam up significantly. Strain the whey to remove any solids. Add the sugar and honey, and stir until they are dissolved, about 5 minutes. Wash down the inside of the pot twice with a pastry brush dipped in water.

3   Increase the heat to medium high and bring the mixture to a boil—this is when it expands. For chewy caramels, cook and stir frequently until the caramel temperature registers 250°F (120°C) on a thermometer, 15 to 20 minutes. (If you clip your thermometer to the pot, make sure the thermometer tip isn't touching the bottom or side of the pot.)

4   When the desired temperature is reached, remove the pot from the heat and stir in the butter and vanilla. Butter an 8-inch square pan and pour the mixture into it. Sprinkle salt on top to taste, if using. Let cool completely, 2 to 3 hours.

5   Once cooled, cut the caramels into 1-inch squares and wrap in waxed paper.

Caramels will keep at room temperature for 2 weeks.

Variations

Instead of wrapping bite-size caramels as Linda suggests, you could do what I tried and make deliciously decadent candy bars by coating slabs of caramel with melted chocolate and chopped nuts.

Cooking the mixture to a lower temperature will produce sauce instead of candy. If you would prefer a caramel sauce, cook until the thermometer registers 235°F (113°C).

Coffee Frappé

This creamy blended coffee drink is easy to whip up when you need a café-style pick-me-up in your own home. The craving is contagious though, so if anyone else is around, prepare to make enough to share. The recipe makes it easy to multiply servings. The mix of nut butter, whey, and instant coffee granules blends into a perfect frappé. You can use decaf granules if you want to enjoy this without the buzz.

Customize flavors just like a barista by sweetening with maple syrup, honey, or flavored syrup and by adding cocoa powder, ground cinnamon, vanilla extract, or anything else you can dream up.

YIELD 1 serving

INGREDIENTS

- 2 cups ice or frozen whey cubes

- 1 cup whey

- 3 tablespoons maple syrup or other sweetener

- 1 tablespoon instant coffee or espresso granules

- 1 tablespoon smooth almond butter or hazelnut butter

WHICH WHEY?
BEST Sweet
GOOD Cooked

1 Add all the ingredients to a blender and blend, starting at medium speed and then processing at high speed until the drink comes together. It should look fluffy and lighter in color. Depending on the processing power of your blender, you might have to use fewer ice cubes or add a little more whey; make sure the blender is off before putting your hand inside, and use a tamper if you have one.

2 Taste and add more maple syrup if you want it sweeter. Blend to combine.

Serve in a tall glass and enjoy immediately.

For extra flavor, freeze whey in ice cube trays and use whey ice cubes instead of regular ice. Be sure to taste the whey first to make sure it's mild and milky.

Vanilla Poached Pears

This recipe was inspired by the French dessert poire belle Hélène. In my version, the pears are luxuriously poached in whey that has been infused with a vanilla bean and lemon rind. That already sounds amazing, right? But then you serve these gorgeous pears with No-Churn Ice Cream (page 105), Hot Fudge Sauce (page 106), *and* whipped cream!

That may seem like a lot of fuss for a pear, but the result is fully worth it. As a bonus, the poaching liquid turns into a pear-infused syrup that you can add to cocktails or seltzer or use to enhance rice pudding, sorbets, granitas, and other desserts.

YIELD 4 servings ••• **TIME** 2 hours, 30 minutes active

INGREDIENTS

- 4 pears
- 2 cups sugar
- 4–6 cups whey
- ½ vanilla bean, split and scraped, or 2 teaspoons vanilla extract
- 3-inch piece lemon zest
- No-Churn Ice Cream (page 105) or other vanilla ice cream for serving, optional
- Unsweetened whipped cream for serving, optional
- Hot Fudge Sauce (page 106) or other chocolate sauce for serving, optional

WHICH WHEY?
BEST Cooked
GOOD Sweet, acid

1 Use a small measuring spoon or melon baller to scoop the seeds out of the pears from the bottom. Peel the pears and trim the stems, keeping at least ½ inch.

2 Whisk the sugar into 4 cups whey in a medium pot until it is dissolved. Add the vanilla bean seeds and pod and lemon zest, then add the peeled pears. The pears should be covered by the whey; if not, add a little more. Put the pot on the stove and simmer over medium-low heat until the pears are fork-tender but not mushy, 15 minutes.

3 Remove the pears from the liquid and transfer them to the refrigerator to cool completely. You can make them a day in advance.

4 To serve with the full poire belle Hélène treatment, stand each pear upright on a plate, place a small scoop of vanilla ice cream next to it, and top with a dollop of unsweetened whipped cream. Serve it with hot fudge sauce or other delicious chocolate sauce on the side.

Make a striking gift by putting a pear in a clear jar and covering it with simple syrup (made by simmering the poaching liquid until it is reduced by half). Include instructions on how to serve the pear and a couple of serving suggestions for the syrup, such as making a champagne cocktail or flavored seltzer.

Jiggly "Apple Pie"

You will either irritate traditionalists or delight playful people with this apple pie–flavored gelatin. There's no baking involved, and people avoiding gluten can enjoy this dish whenever they crave the flavors of apple pie. This unconventional dessert sure is fun to eat, and it's a far cry from boxed gelatin mixes with artificial colors and flavors. Made with apple juice and whey, it's a wholesome, satisfying, and refreshing treat that melts in the mouth.

YIELD 8 servings ••• **TIME** 4 hours, 20 minutes active

INGREDIENTS

- 2 cups apple juice or apple cider
- 2 tablespoons unflavored gelatin
- 1 large apple, peeled, cored, and thinly sliced
- ¼ cup honey or maple syrup
- 1 teaspoon lemon juice
- ½ teaspoon ground cinnamon
- 2 cups whey
- Whipped cream for serving
- Toasted pecans for serving

WHICH WHEY?
BEST Sweet, cooked
GOOD Acid

1. Place ½ cup of the apple juice in a bowl and add the gelatin to bloom it. Whisk until the mixture looks a little like applesauce.

2. Add the apple slices to a pot with the remaining 1½ cups juice. Bring to a quick boil until the apple slices just wilt, not fall apart. Remove from the heat.

3. Remove the apple slices from the juice, letting them drain a little, and place them in a pie plate.

4. Whisk the bloomed gelatin mixture into the hot juice in the pot and stir to fully dissolve the gelatin. Add the honey, lemon juice, and cinnamon, and whisk thoroughly. Stir in the whey. Taste for sweetness and add more honey if needed.

5. Pour the gelatin mixture over the apples. When the slices rise to the surface, arrange them as desired. Place the pie plate in the refrigerator and allow to set for at least 3 hours or until fully firm.

6. To serve, cut into slices (it will be firmer than conventional gelatin), and top each serving with a dollop of whipped cream and a few pecans. To unmold the whole pie before slicing it, dip the bottom of the pie plate into warm (not hot) water for 30 seconds at a time until you see the pie loosening around the edges. Watch carefully to avoid overmelting the gelatin. Place a serving platter over the pan and flip.

Store in the refrigerator and enjoy within 5 days.

Upside-Down Lime and Coconut Pie

This curious pie forms its own top crust with the shredded coconut as it bakes, as if it had been flipped. The coconut gets toasty and crunchy, and you have to crack it to get to the lime-and-whey custard underneath. I respect a dessert that performs tricks, especially one that's this easy to make. No need to roll dough or fix a water bath, just blend, pour, and bake. The only difficult part of this recipe is waiting for the pie to chill completely before you dig in.

YIELD 8 servings ••• **TIME** 3 hours, 15 minutes active

INGREDIENTS

- 2 cups whey
- ¾ cup sugar
- ½ cup butter, melted
- ½ cup all-purpose flour
- 4 large eggs
- 2 teaspoons grated lime zest
- ½ cup lime juice
- 1 teaspoon vanilla extract
- 1 cup unsweetened shredded coconut

WHICH WHEY?
BEST Sweet
GOOD Acid
OKAY Cooked

1 Preheat the oven to 350°F (180°C). Butter and flour a 9-inch pie plate.

2 Add the whey, sugar, butter, flour, eggs, lime zest, lime juice, and vanilla to a blender and process until smooth.

3 Add the coconut and pulse a couple of times, just enough to incorporate it.

4 Pour the batter into the prepared pie plate and bake for 45 to 50 minutes. The center will be set, but still slightly wobbly. The top should be dry and golden.

5 Let the pie cool completely, then refrigerate it for at least 2 hours or overnight.

Store in the refrigerator and enjoy within 5 days.

You can change up the citrus in this pie however you like. I like to make it with Meyer lemons, and I bet it would be amazing with passion fruit. It's always delicious served with whipped cream.

Natillas de Canela
(Mexican Cinnamon Pudding Cups)

Pudding was one of the few desserts my Nana Julia made when I was a child, and the flavor of cinnamon is especially comforting and nostalgic. She would let me drink the pudding mixture before it set because it's a lot like Mexican atole or champurrado, which are thick, warm drinks. If you've never tried warm pudding, I encourage you to do so!

I think she would approve of my whey version, with the addition of orange rind. I just love the flavor combination of cinnamon and orange, popular in both Mexico and Spain. Whether you infuse the whey with these flavors or with lemon rind, cardamom, or cocoa powder, you'll end up with lovely natillas.

YIELD 6 servings ••• **TIME** 25 minutes

INGREDIENTS

- 1 large orange
- 4 cups whey
- 1 large cinnamon stick, preferably canela*
- 4 large egg yolks
- ⅔ cup sugar or other granulated sweetener of your choice
- ⅓ cup cornstarch
- 1 tablespoon butter or ghee
  Ground cinnamon
- 6 Mexican tea biscuits or other plain cookies, optional

*See What Is Mexican Cinnamon?, page 37.

WHICH WHEY?
BEST Any type

1. Remove the zest from the orange, avoiding any white pith. Add the whey, cinnamon stick, and orange zest to a 2-quart pot and set over medium heat until the mixture reaches a boil. Continue to cook for 15 minutes. Remove from the heat and allow to cool for 30 minutes.

2. Meanwhile, whisk the egg yolks with the sugar. Add the cornstarch and mix well until smooth. Set aside.

3. Line a fine-mesh strainer with a double layer of fine-mesh cheesecloth. Pour the cooled whey through the strainer into another heavy pot.

4. Add ½ cup of the cooled whey to the egg yolk mixture and whisk until smooth again. Pour this mixture into the pot of whey and stir thoroughly to incorporate.

5   Cook over medium heat, stirring constantly to avoid sticking at the bottom of the pot as the pudding thickens. This should take about 10 minutes. When it reaches a boil, continue to cook and stir for 1 minute longer. Remove from the heat.

6   Turn off the heat and stir in the butter until fully melted and incorporated. Ladle warm pudding into six small bowls. Enjoy natillas warm or put the bowls in the refrigerator to cool and set. Before serving, sprinkle with ground cinnamon and top with a cookie, if using.

Store in the refrigerator and enjoy within 4 days.

The addition of a simple tea biscuit on top of pudding is a traditional Mexican touch. The ones used in Mexico are called Marias. You can find them in the Latin foods aisle in most grocery stores. They soften a little but add a nice texture as you dig into your pudding. If you can't find Mexican tea biscuits, use your favorite cookies and feel free to layer them with added fruit for a parfait-style dessert.

APPENDIX

Whey Nutrient Profiles

In these charts, I've listed the most notable nutrients present in a quart of either sweet whey or acid whey. Cooked whey (from ricotta, for example) contains less fat, fewer calories, less protein, and fewer vitamins and minerals overall, so I didn't include it.

You can scale the values down by the cup or up to a full gallon. There are several other nutrients present in smaller amounts.

These nutrients are based on cow's milk whey and will vary by the animal source and the process used to get the whey. The only way of finding out the exact nutrient content of the whey from your animals' or purchased milk would be to have it tested by a lab. Then the findings would apply only to that particular batch of whey, produced on that day.

For comparison purposes, I also included information on milk nutrients, dried whey, and a powdered whey product. In the charts on the pages that follow, I compared sweet whey to these other nutrient sources because it's generally the most widely produced type of whey in both home-based and large-scale operations.

Note: I gathered much of this information from the USDA's FoodData Central website (http://fdc.nal.usda.gov). To see more about whey nutrient values on the site, enter "whey" as a search term, click on SNR Legacy Foods, and choose sweet or acid whey. I also used SELF NutritionData (https://nutritiondata.self.com). To see whey nutrition information translated into measures like glycemic index and Percent Daily Value, enter "whey" as a search term and choose sweet or acid whey.

Nutrient Content of Liquid Sweet Whey and Liquid Acid Whey

It's very interesting to see the similarities and differences in the nutrient profiles of sweet whey from making cheese and acid whey from drained yogurt. Kefir is a bit of an outlier since it isn't usually drained for its whey. While no nutrient information on kefir whey is available, we can assume it's closest to acid whey drained from yogurt.

NUTRIENT	SWEET WHEY, 1 QUART (984 grams by weight)	ACID WHEY, 1 QUART (984 grams by weight)
WATER	916 grams	919 grams
ENERGY/CALORIES	226 kilocalories	236 kilocalories
PROTEIN	8.36 grams	7.48 grams
TOTAL FAT	3.54 grams	0.886 grams
SUGARS	50.6 grams (lactose)	50.4 grams (lactose)
CARBOHYDRATE	50.6 grams	50.4 grams
CHOLESTEROL	19.7 milligrams	9.84 milligrams
CALCIUM	462 milligrams	1010 milligrams
MAGNESIUM	78.7 milligrams	98.4 milligrams
PHOSPHORUS	453 milligrams	768 milligrams
POTASSIUM	1580 milligrams	1410 milligrams
SODIUM	531 milligrams	472 milligrams
CHOLINE	157 milligrams	157 milligrams
ASPARTIC ACID	0.817 grams	0.728 grams
GLUTAMIC ACID	1.46 grams	1.34 grams
ZINC	1.28 milligrams	4.23 milligrams
FOLATE	9.84 micrograms	19.7 micrograms
SELENIUM	19.7 micrograms	17.7 micrograms
RIBOFLAVIN	1.56 milligrams	1.38 milligrams
VITAMIN B$_{12}$	2.76 micrograms	1.77 micrograms
VITAMIN RAE/RETINOL	29.5 micrograms	19.7 micrograms
VITAMIN A	118 International Units (IU)	68.9 International Units (IU)

Nutrient Content of Liquid Sweet Whey and Liquid Whole Milk

This chart shows what is lost and what is retained when we make cheese and the differences between the nutrient profiles of sweet whey and whole milk.

NUTRIENT	SWEET WHEY, 1 QUART (984 grams by weight)	WHOLE COW'S MILK, 1 QUART (996 grams by weight)
WATER	916 grams	996 grams
ENERGY/CALORIES	226 kilocalories	608 kilocalories
PROTEIN	8.36 grams	32.56 grams
TOTAL FAT	3.54 grams	27.6 grams
SUGARS	50.6 grams (lactose)	48 grams (lactose)
CARBOHYDRATE	50.6 grams	46 grams
CHOLESTEROL	19.7 milligrams	119.6 milligrams
CALCIUM	462 milligrams	1224 milligrams
MAGNESIUM	78.7 milligrams	118.4 milligrams
PHOSPHORUS	453 milligrams	1004 milligrams
POTASSIUM	1580 milligrams	1496 milligrams
SODIUM	531 milligrams	378.4 milligrams
CHOLINE	157 milligrams	177.2 milligrams
ASPARTIC ACID	0.817 grams	2.78 grams
GLUTAMIC ACID	1.46 grams	7.84 grams
ZINC	1.28 milligrams	4.2 milligrams
FOLATE	9.84 micrograms	0 micrograms*
SELENIUM	19.7 micrograms	18.92 micrograms
RIBOFLAVIN	1.56 milligrams	1.376 milligrams
VITAMIN B$_{12}$	2.76 micrograms	5.36 micrograms
VITAMIN RAE/RETINOL	29.5 micrograms	Vitamin A, RAE 318.8 micrograms**
VITAMIN A	118 International Units (IU)	Retinol 308.8 micrograms**

*The reported lack of folate in whole milk doesn't make sense, but is based on 12 samples from different sources that were tested by the Department of Agriculture. This testing showed that samples of low-fat milk contained an average of 2 micrograms folate per cup and as much as 7 micrograms per cup.

**Vitamin A and retinol were reported in a different format in milk vs whey.

Nutrient Content of Liquid Sweet Whey and Whey Protein Powder Product

This comparison shows how the kind of liquid sweet whey you can produce at home when making cheese stacks up against the commercially produced whey protein powders sold as supplements to bodybuilders and other people seeking a protein boost. Brand-name protein powders like the one used in this comparison usually contain flavorings, such as a low-calorie sweetener (or sometimes just sugar), and may have other nutrients added and subtracted.

You will often hear that whey is high in protein. While there is some protein in liquid whey, there is a lot more in whey powder because dehydrating the whey concentrates the protein content. Interestingly, liquid whey compares favorably to protein powder on many micronutrient levels despite its high water content.

NUTRIENT	LIQUID SWEET WHEY, 1 QUART (984 grams by weight)	WHEY PROTEIN POWDER, 3 SCOOPS (86 grams by weight)
WATER	916 grams	0 grams
ENERGY/CALORIES	226 kilocalories	309 kilocalories
PROTEIN	8.36 grams	50 grams
TOTAL FAT	3.54 grams	998 grams
SUGARS	50.6 grams (lactose)	71 grams
CARBOHYDRATE	50.6 grams	25 grams
CHOLESTEROL	19.7 milligrams	10.3 milligrams
CALCIUM	462 milligrams	600 milligrams
MAGNESIUM	78.7 milligrams	200 milligrams
PHOSPHORUS	453 milligrams	500 milligrams
POTASSIUM	1580 milligrams	750 milligrams
SODIUM	531 milligrams	320 milligrams
CHOLINE	157 milligrams	157 milligrams
ASPARTIC ACID	0.817 grams	0.817 grams
GLUTAMIC ACID	1.46 grams	46 grams
ZINC	1.28 milligrams	7.5 milligrams
FOLATE	9.84 micrograms	200 micrograms
SELENIUM	19.7 micrograms	35 micrograms
RIBOFLAVIN	1.56 milligrams	0.85 milligrams
VITAMIN B$_{12}$	2.76 micrograms	3 micrograms*
VITAMIN RAE/RETINOL	29.5 micrograms	750 micrograms
VITAMIN A	118 International Units (IU)	2500 International Units (IU)

*Vitamin B$_{12}$ was labeled as added on the protein powder label. Vitamin E (not shown) was also added.

Nutrient Content of Liquid Sweet Whey and Dehydrated Sweet Whey

This chart compares the nutrient content of liquid sweet whey derived from making cheese to that of dried sweet whey powder. This type of powder is the kind that's often added to packaged foods such as cookies, crackers, and cheese puffs to name just a few. The powder is simply spray-dried whey with nothing added. Dried whey is different from whey-based protein powders that may have nutrients added and subtracted. It's enlightening to see how some of these values compare to those of liquid whey.

NUTRIENT	LIQUID SWEET WHEY, 1 QUART (984 grams by weight)	DEHYDRATED SWEET WHEY, 1 CUP SCOOP (145 grams by weight)
WATER	916 grams	0 grams
ENERGY/CALORIES	226 kilocalories	512 kilocalories
PROTEIN	8.36 grams	18.7 grams
TOTAL FAT	3.54 grams	1.55 grams
SUGARS	50.6 grams (lactose)	108 grams
CARBOHYDRATE	50.6 grams	108 grams
CHOLESTEROL	19.7 milligrams	8.7 milligrams
CALCIUM	462 milligrams	1150 milligrams
MAGNESIUM	78.7 milligrams	255 milligrams
PHOSPHORUS	453 milligrams	1350 milligrams
POTASSIUM	1580 milligrams	3020 milligrams
SODIUM	531 milligrams	1570 milligrams
CHOLINE	157 milligrams	326 milligrams
ASPARTIC ACID	.817 grams	1.84 grams
GLUTAMIC ACID	1.46 grams	3.26 grams
ZINC	1.28 milligrams	2.86 milligrams
FOLATE	9.84 micrograms	17.4 micrograms
SELENIUM	19.7 micrograms	39.4 micrograms
RIBOFLAVIN	1.56 milligrams	3.2 milligrams
VITAMIN B$_{12}$	2.76 micrograms	3.44 micrograms
VITAMIN RAE/RETINOL	29.5 micrograms	Vitamin RAE/Retinol 11.6 micrograms
VITAMIN A	118 International Units (IU)	Vitamin A 43.5 International Units (IU)

Nutrient Content of Dehydrated Sweet Whey and Dehydrated Deproteinized Whey (Cooked Whey)

And finally, this chart gives us an idea of the nutrients left in cooked whey from ricotta or other high-heat acid-coagulated cheeses with no added rennet and how the nutrient content of this type of whey compares to that of dried sweet whey. Complete nutritional information is not as readily available for dried cooked whey because it's used almost exclusively as a food additive. The values that are missing are not reported, but we can get an idea of the breakdown by the nutrients listed below.

NUTRIENT	DEHYDRATED SWEET WHEY, 1 CUP SCOOP (145 grams by weight)	DEPROTEINIZED WHEY POWDER (100 grams by weight)
ENERGY/CALORIES	512 kilocalories	351 kilocalories
PROTEIN	18.7 grams	3.6 grams
TOTAL FAT	1.55 grams	0 grams
SUGARS	108 grams	78 grams
CARBOHYDRATE	108 grams	82.6 grams
CHOLESTEROL	8.7 milligrams	1 milligram
CALCIUM	1150 milligrams	584 milligrams
MAGNESIUM	255 milligrams	
PHOSPHORUS	1350 milligrams	
POTASSIUM	3020 milligrams	2170 milligrams
SODIUM	1570 milligrams	675 milligrams
CHOLINE	326 milligrams	
ASPARTIC ACID	1.84 grams	
GLUTAMIC ACID	3.26 grams	
ZINC	2.86 milligrams	
FOLATE	17.4 micrograms	
SELENIUM	39.4 micrograms	
RIBOFLAVIN	3.2 milligrams	
VITAMIN B$_{12}$	3.44 micrograms	
VITAMIN RAE/RETINOL	11.6 micrograms	
VITAMIN A	43.5 IU (International Units)	

Acknowledgments

A most heartfelt round of applause to the incredible people who managed to contribute to this book despite the events and extra weight of 2020 and 2021. For the texts, emails, calls, video messages, Zoom chats, and backyard masked meetings, thank you: Heather Arndt-Anderson, Linda Bangs, Gianaclis Caldwell, Hannah Crum, Emily Darchuk, Nicole Easterday, Ashley English, Rita Gonsalves, Sarah Marshall, Leta Merrill, Lee Ann Moyer, Kirsten Shockey, Eddie and Laura Valtierra, Noemy Vera, Gwynnie Vernon, and Cathy Whims.

A big thank-you to Jeff, who encouraged a healthy sleeping schedule and checked to make sure I was drinking enough water while I wrote this book.

Much appreciation, as always, to friends and family who stop hearing from me when a deadline is approaching. Your understanding and support mean so much!

To the creators of the entertaining, informative, and inspiring books, podcasts, YouTube channels, and TV shows that provided a balance to the news and hard work during this time, I owe a lot of my sanity to you. Thank you. Your art, comedy, advice, and expertise make a difference!

Index

Numbers in **bold** indicate tables.

EXPLORE THE WORLD OF
CHEESEMAKING
with More Books from Storey

INSTANT POT CHEESE
by Claudia Lucero

Make cheese in your Instant Pot! With this expert guide, you can create your own ricotta, mozzarella, queso blanco, burrata, cottage cheese, cream cheese, feta, sour cream, mascarpone, and much more. Dairy-free options include Smoky Coconut Melter, Tangy Crumbler, and American Cheddar 'n' Chives Wheel.

HOME CHEESE MAKING, 4th Edition
by Ricki Carroll

This handbook covers it all, from timeless classics like mozzarella and cheddar to sophisticated options such as halloumi, raclette, and gorgonzola. It also includes 50 delicious recipes for cooking with your homemade cheese.

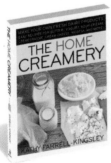

THE HOME CREAMERY
by Kathy Farrell-Kingsley

It's easy to make your own butter, yogurt, sour cream, and more! Step-by-step instructions make it simple, and 75 delicious recipes—from Apple Coffee Cake to Zucchini Triangles—help you showcase your freshly made dairy.

JOIN THE CONVERSATION. Share your experience with this book, learn more about Storey Publishing's authors, and read original essays and book excerpts at storey.com. Look for our books wherever quality books are sold or call 800-441-5700.